Discov
Coastal Lancashire

RON & MARLENE FREETHY

JOHN DONALD PUBLISHERS LTD
EDINBURGH

ISBN 0 85976 335 8

British Library Cataloguing in Publication Data
Freethy, Ron
   Discovering Lancashire.
   1. The coast
   1. Lancashire (England). Travel
   I. Title II. Freethy, Marlene
   914.2760859

Phototypeset by Newtext Composition Ltd, Glasgow.
Printed & bound in Great Britain by Scotprint Ltd, Musselburgh.

Introduction

Both of us were born in the county of Lancashire, although the boundary changes of 1974 made one of us a Cumbrian as the Furness district was absorbed. Like all young north-westerners we were taken to the seaside and at the time didn't know how lucky we were to have the best fun resorts in Britain at our fingertips. In those days the rail network was extensive, not too expensive and usually reliable.

Thus we have enjoyed writing this book about Lancashire's coastline but we are conscious of offending some modernists who point to Merseyside as a county. We make no apology. We love Liverpool but it *is* in Lancashire. Without its vibrant energy there would have been no import and export of textiles and no industrial revolution which was spawned in the inland towns which we describe in a companion volume.

Writers need help and encouragement. We are grateful to Robert Smithies with whom we have worked on several television films, particularly concerning the rivers Lune, Wyre, Ribble and Mersey. We are pleased to include two of his Liverpool photographs in this book.

Finally we wish to thank our son Paul who frequently misquotes *The Importance of Being Ernest* when asked about his parents: 'To lose one parent in pursuit of research can be considered to be unfortunate but to lose both in the production of one book is unforgivable.'

In our best Lankie accent we say 'Sorry Lad', and to him we dedicate this book.

Acknowledgement

The cover illustration of Fleetwood Dock is reproduced by permission of Bill Wilkinson, Press Photographer, Fulwood, Preston.

Contents

	Page
Introduction	v
1. Liverpool and Merseyside	1
2. Southport and the Ribble Estuary	25
3. Blackpool and the Fylde	44
4. Fleetwood and the River Wyre	66
5. Lunesdale to Lancaster and the Sea	90
6. Around Morecambe and Heysham	115
7. Morecambe Bay	126
Further Reading	144
Index	145

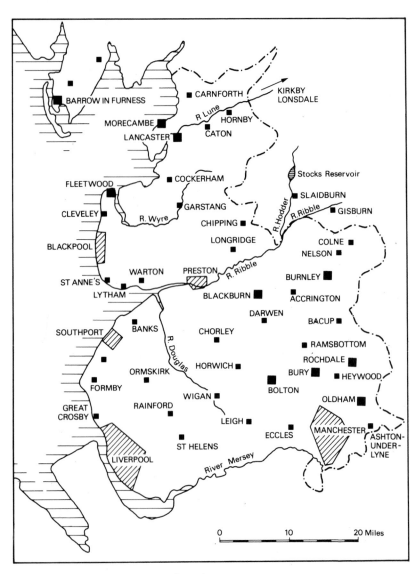

Location map

CHAPTER 1

Liverpool and Merseyside

Lancashire's coastline has long been dominated by the mighty Port of Liverpool and there can be only one place to begin an exploration of the old county seascape. We have a fondness for the city which, like most friendships, was slow to develop but which, once established, will endure for ever. Liverpool has a unique spirit, but finding it is a lifetime's work.

We have stood on the Kop at Anfield and watched the Reds of Liverpool do battle with the Blues of Everton. Is this the spirit of Liverpool? Not quite. We have read of the polarised disagreements between the far left reds and the beleaguered blues in one of the most impressive Town Halls in Europe. Is this the spirit of Liverpool? Nowhere near! Over the years we have listened to, watched and even talked to Liverpudlian comics such as Arthur Askey, Ted Ray, Tommy Handley, Ken Dodd the Diddyman from Knotty Ash and Jimmy Tarbuck. Are they the spirits of Liverpool? Almost! In our comparative youth we have crushed into the Cavern Club and listened to the Beatles. Is this the elusive spirit? Partly! We have for many years given the bookmakers our hard-earned cash on one Saturday in March when Aintree hosts the world's greatest steeplechase. The race over 4 miles and 856 yards separated by around 30 jumps began at Maghull near Ormskirk in 1837 before moving to Aintree the year after. Is this the spirit of Liverpool? Probably not! Where is this spirit, then? Could it be served in the bars of one of the Victorian hotels which once hosted those on passage between England and North America in the days of the transatlantic liners? Maybe. The real answer, however, is that all the ingredients listed above and many others are blended together to produce the spirit of the city which intoxicates us. We cannot drink enough of it!

No city or seaport in Britain has been so maligned as Liverpool although the majority of its critics have never been to the place and know nothing of and care even less for its vibrant history or its magnificent architecture. Its citizens have every right to feel proud of their city. We feel that the best way to discover the spirit of Liverpool is to climb aboard one of the Mersey Ferries. Actually the Ferry service across the River is even older than Liverpool itself and was actually more important to the early residents of the Wirral in Cheshire than to the Lancastrians. Seacombe Ferry is mentioned in the Domesday Book. In 1150 Hamo de Massey, the third Baron of Dunham, granted an area of land in the Wirral to the Benedictine monks who built Birkenhead Priory, the ruins of which still stand and are overlooked by the often troubled Cammel Laird's shipyard. The monks were allowed to raise revenue from the ferry, and there is much documentary evidence to support its existence. Rowing across the Mersey, especially in stormy weather, was a distinct hazard. In 1330 Edward III confirmed the ferry charter allowing the monks to carry 'men and horses and all other things whatsoever'. Which was the earliest ferry route is not known for certain but there were crossings to New Brighton, Egremont, Seacombe, Woodside and Birkenhead, which was usually called the Monks Ferry, Tranmere, Rock Ferry, the New Ferry and Eastham. As the population of the Wirral and of Liverpool itself increased, the demand for the ferry services also increased.

Following the dissolution of Birkenhead Priory in 1536, the Ferry rights were bought by one Ralph Worsley, but there were then several owners until 1835 when the Woodside, North Birkenhead and Liverpool Steam Ferry Company was formed, but it proved not to be viable and in 1839 was bought by the Birkenhead and Chester Railway Company. The operating problems were still not solved, however, and Birkenhead Council took over to keep the route open in 1842. Some loss of revenue resulted from the opening of the under-river railway service in 1885, which was five years earlier than the London tube. Yet another first for Merseyside! The profits were thereafter good and continued until the first Mersey Road Tunnel was opened by King George V in July 1934. This prefaced a disaster for the ferries and in particular for the so-called Woodside luggage boat, which despite its name was

Pier Head from the Maritime Museum.

actually a car ferry. The effect of the road tunnel on this service had obviously been foreseen before building ever commenced and a compromise agreement had been reached whereby the road tunnel would subsidise the ferries for 21 years. No doubt the coming of the second world war accelerated the closure of the luggage ferry in 1941, but in 1955 a further 19 years of subsidy was agreed. In 1974 the Merseyside County Council took over the running of the Ferry. After many years of pretending that the river route was as important as the tunnel, it has at last been accepted that the ferry is more viable as a tourist attraction. In the early 1990s vessels were refurbished and began to offer comfortable river cruises as well as a scenic crossing to New Brighton, which is also beginning to reassert itself as one of the North West's seaside resorts. Visitors to the Wirral are also able to visit Liverpool without having to worry about parking.

This is in fact our favourite route into Liverpool as it gives us a chance to appreciate the comparative speed of the tunnels as well as providing the invigoration of a short sea trip. Approaching Pier Head from the river, you can see just how compact the street pattern of Liverpool is and how easy it is to explore its magnificent buildings.

Although there was only a cluster of huts around the liver-coloured muddy pool in 1207, it still attracted King John who founded the town. He thus signed the Liverpool charter some eight years before he bowed to the demands of the Barons and signed Magna Carta. John was not noted for his good deeds, so why was he so good to Liverpool? The answer was Ireland which John wished to conquer and he needed a port from which to launch an invasion. He had attempted to use Milford Haven but the Welsh were being difficult, and Chester, which would have been the next obvious choice, was owned by the Earl of Chester and John's dealings with his Earls in pre-Magna Carta days was anything but friendly. So Liverpool was the third choice, and even this bit of exposed land had to be prized away from Henry Fitzwarine by the offer of a much larger area of prime land near Preston.

To supply the small port and its troops a network of seven streets radiated from the harbour and these are still the main thoroughfares to this day even though names may have

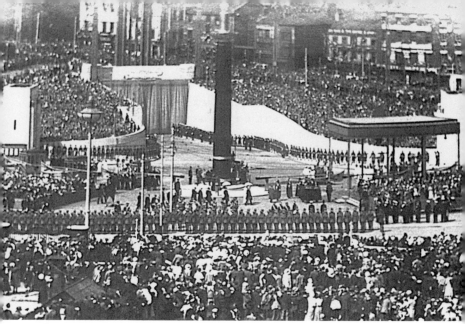

King Georve V opening the Mersey Tunnel linking Liverpool with Birkenhead in July 1934, the first link.

changed over the centuries. Castle Street ran from King John's Fortress which stood on the site where the Queen Victoria monument now stands. There are drawings of the castle, but there is actually a model built on the banks of the Rivington reservoirs near Bolton by Thomas Lister who made his fortune from Sunlight soap and whose model village and factory are at Port Sunlight on the Wirral bank of the Mersey. There was also Chapel Street on which still stands the parish church which was initially governed from the much older Ormskirk. There was also Dale Street, Mill Street, which in the sixteenth century was renamed Old Hall Street, with Moor Street becoming Tithebarn Street and Bank Street becoming Water Street. There was also a Juggler Street which kept its name until the eighteenth century when it was renamed High Street and then swallowed up by Exchange Flags. In medieval times street entertainers earned a living on Juggler Street and here perhaps were the ancestors of the Askeys, Handleys, Tarbucks, Rays and Doddy's Diddymen!

Although King John provided the initial impetus, Liverpool developed slowly and was not an important port until the sixteenth century, up to which time it was regarded as a mere creek and under the control of Chester. It was, however, used by the Earl of Derby who was also the Lord of the Isle of Man. In fact it was not until 1658 during the Commonwealth that Livepool became a port in its own right, this despite its support for the King during the Civil Wars. Perhaps it was accepted by Cromwell that when Colonel Ralph Assheton took the town in May 1643 it would not have been possible without some assistance from those within. In June 1644 Prince Rupert was ousted from Liverpool with great loss of life to both his army and the local people. When the Prince recaptured Liverpool his troops treated the population very badly. We once made the mistake in the presence of a historian of the period of saying that Liverpool was an unimportant skirmish but he firmly pointed out that the expenditure of hundreds of barrels of gunpowder and around 2,000 casualties contributed to Prince Rupert's defeat at Marston Moor near York later in the month. Perhaps this was why Cromwell had a soft spot for Liverpool.

Another important historical event then took a hand – the settlement of America by the Pilgrim Fathers and later the occupation of the West Indies. These were best reached from England's west-coast ports and Liverpool was ideal for the import of tobacco, sugar and later cotton. By the end of the seventeenth century it became obvious that the Pool would have to be developed and given more protection. By 1715, after pioneering work by George Sorrocold and Thomas Steers, the first commercial wet dock in Britain was opened, with Steers as the first manager.

Lancashire's textile manufacturers were not slow to realise the potential of the port, and out went woollen and later cotton fabrics and in came sugar, spices, rum, tobacco and raw cotton. Initially Liverpool was not involved in the slave trade but by 1760 this then legal but infamous business had been wrested from London and Bristol and 69 Liverpool ships were engaged in what became known as the triangular voyage. This meant that each vessel would be away from its home port for up to one year. Manufactured goods and cowrie shells which were used as currency were taken to West Africa and exchanged for slaves; these unfortunates were taken to the West Indies and America where they were sold, usually in exchange for cotton, molasses, sugar and rum.

By 1807 Liverpool was all-powerful, having become known

Classifying cotton in the Liverpool Exchange during the 1950s.

as the Port of a Thousand Ships, and even the abolition of the lucrative slave trade in 1807 did little to affect its growing prosperity. It should be said that many Liverpool merchants were vociferous in their condemnation of the slave trade and William Roscoe and William Rathbone were staunch supporters of William Wilberforce whose name is for ever associated with its abolition.

There were many merchants who spent some of their profits on embellishing the town which eventually resulted in Liverpool gaining city status in 1880, and in 1893 Queen Victoria signed a charter allowing the establishment of a Lord Mayor. By this time the population was well in excess of half a million.

Around any important port there have to develop impressive docking and cargo-handling facilities plus other industries which rely on either imports, exports or indeed both. Thus Liverpool became a centre for match making, soap manufacture, flour milling, sugar refining, tobacco processing and oil refining. Liverpool was a boom city and its buildings reflect this.

The Town Hall was first built in 1754 but was rebuilt following a fire in 1807, a structure of impressive style and proportions set at the junction of Dale Street, Castle Street and Water Street. Although the council meets in a chamber described by Edward VII as the best proportioned room in Europe with the exception of the Winter Palace in St Petersburg, the building is not actually the base for the city's administration. The municipal offices are in Dale Street, enabling John Wood's Town Hall to be enjoyed by visitors without disrupting the work of the city officers.

Three buildings on the Pier Head are perhaps a major ingredient of the Spirit of Liverpool which we have been searching for. The granite-faced Royal Liver Building, constructed between 1908 and 1911, was the first substantial building in the world to be constructed of reinforced concrete. It is the head office of the Royal Liver Friendly Society but it is more famous for having the largest clock in Britain and also the Liver Birds. The four clock faces have a diameter of 25 feet (7.6 metres) compared to that of Big Ben which is 23 feet (7.1 metres). The building has 17 storeys and a height of 304 feet (93 metres), whilst on the top of the twin domed towers are the Liver Birds measuring 18 feet (5.5 metres) which more than any other objects are the symbol of Liverpool. We reacted with horror in the latter half of 1990 when some local councillors expressed a wish to have a more dignified coat of arms and proposed the removal of the Liver Bird. We wonder what could be more dignified than history and also the obvious fact that the mythical Liver Bird is unique. In 1797 the heraldic description read: 'Argent, a Cormorant in the beak a branch of seaweed called Laver all proper, and for the Crest, on a wreath of colours a Cormorant, the wings elevated, in the beak a branch of Laver proper.'

It is thought that the original seal was lost in the siege of 1644 and the Eagle of St John was then replaced by a poorly drawn cormorant and the fleur-de-lys was replaced by the seaweed. Other cities have eagles and the fleur-de-lys, but none have the cormorant or the seaweed. For a seaport what could

The *Aquitania*, pride of the Cunard fleet at Liverpool in 1914 (Merseyside County Museums).

be better than a seabird and a sprig of seaweed?

Built in 1907, the Port of Liverpool Building is surmounted by a green dome supported on pillars and has a distinctly Venetian look about it. The interior is also impressive and the inner rim of the dome is inscribed with a quotation from the Bible reading 'They that go down to the sea in ships and do business in great waters; these see the works of the Lord and His wonders in the deep.'

The Cunard Building was constructed during the First World War and also has a distinctly Italian feel about it, with some modifications made to reflect the War, including the coats of arms of the Allied Forces which face the pier head and greet those approaching the city from the sea. The Cunard Company ran its Transatlantic business from here but obviously this declined as air travel took over, and since 1978 the company has worked from a smaller office in the city. The building now accommodates the VAT offices, the French Consulate, ICI offices and several other shipping offices which maintain the building's original connection with the sea.

Although its money was generated by tough businessmen, the city never neglected the arts. The Royal Philharmonic Orchestra have a deserved worldwide reputation and when they play at home, especially in St George's Hall, it is an event to be savoured. The magnificent building was designed by Harvey Lonsdale Elmes, as a result of public subscription was begun in 1836 and opened in 1854; its style is a combination of classical Greek and Roman temples set on a plinth, its pale stone reflecting the sunlight. The building has served both as a law court and a concert hall. In late 1990 Prince Charles suggested a restoration scheme for the hall to have it looking at its best for a Columbus exhibition to take place in 1992, but it will probably take much longer than this. With St George's Hall dominating William Brown Street, there can be no better gateway into an area devoted to art, literature and science museums all housed in magnificent buildings. These include the circular and colonnaded Picton Library, the Brown Library, the Walker Art Gallery and the Museum, all built in the late nineteenth century and renovated following the damage and devastation caused by German bombers during the Second World War.

Liverpool has two interesting – some would say magnificent – cathedrals. Both the Anglican and the Catholic Cathedrals stand on high ground and dominate the city. The Anglican building, designed by Sir Gilbert Scott, was begun in 1904 but the first peal of bells did not ring out until 1951, partly because the huge sandstone building needed time and money to reach completion, but also because some delay and damage were caused by the second world war. The mighty tower soars to a height of 466 feet (142 metres) and the cathedral is the largest Anglican church in the world, being twice the size of St Paul's. In contrast to the Gothic style of the Anglican cathedral the Roman Catholic Metropolitan Cathedral is a much more

View from Rock Ferry on the Cheshire Bank showing the Anglican Cathedral on the far right, with 'Paddy's Wigwam' the third building from the right.

modern-looking structure. Designed by Sir Frederick Gibberd, it was consecrated in 1967 and its tent-like shape has resulted in its local name of 'Paddy's Wigwam'.

By the 1970s Liverpool's docks were in a sad state of decline around the Pier Head area as the container traffic was being handled at Seaforth. Fortunately the city's history was commemorated by the opening of the Liverpool Maritime Museum in the old Pilotage Headquarters at Pier Head which has a substantial visitors' car park alongside. In the late 1980s a branch of the Tate Gallery in London was opened overlooking Pier Head. It is fitting in Liverpool that this should originally have been funded with money made from the import and processing of sugar. The Old Customs House is now the nerve centre for Granada TV's news operation, and other old buildings now house exclusive arcaded shops, cafes and walkways. The museum itself has impressive indoor and outdoor displays. There is an industrial trail which takes in the Albert Dock, built in the 1840s and now restored, as is the Senhouse Dock which was in use between the wars. There is a full-size replica of a traditional Liverpool pilot schooner which is actually seaworthy, as many young people can bear excited witness. Inside is a scale model of the *Titanic* which sank on her maiden voyage in 1912, and also a painfully accurate mock-up of a slave ship, as well as vessels which took emigrants to America during periods of economic depression. There are many displays including audio-visual presentations, a large bookshop and a comfortable restaurant. There is a display devoted to the Leeds to Liverpool Canal, but there is also a developing display of canal life situated at Stanley Dock on the way out of the city towards Bootle.

We enjoyed a magnificent day here in early April when we watched a peregrine falcon soaring among some dilapidated warehouses and causing chaos among the resident pigeons. We were looking for the terminus of the Leeds to Liverpool Canal which is in Stanley Dock. The Maritime Museum has, quite rightly, received a lot of favourable publicity, but to our mind the events evolving around Stanley Dock are just as exciting as the canal was the link between the seaport and the huge industrial complexes of Lancashire and Yorkshire. Here are the old warehouses where tobacco, cotton, wool and sugar were all stored prior to being moved or while awaiting the payment of import dues. At the end of the dock is a chimney which carried fumes from the furnace in which the tobacco sweepings and leaves from burst sacks were burned and which became known as the King's Pipe. The Mersey Heritage Centre organises dockside entertainments, especially at Christmas and in May. During the Christmas Past Weekend, entertainments include jugglers, uni-cyclists, fire eaters, Morris dancers, brass bands, folk groups and singers, clowns, jesters, puppeteers and clog dancers plus traditional dock road musicians whose predecessors once entertained sailors and canal bargees. An array of side shows and exhibitions, slide shows and short lectures provide facts in an easy-to-digest manner. Local crafts are sold at pocket-money prices and there are roulette and roll-a-penny stalls plus coconut shies and tombola. Roast pig, potatoes and chestnuts plus cauldrons of hot spicy fruit punch

Stanley dock, with the entrance to the Leeds to Liverpool Canal just to the right of the two boats. How congested this must have been when this was the Port's only access to the large inland markets.

ensure the real Christmas flavour of old Liverpool. In May a similar exhibition is organised except that there are more outdoor events including carthorses at work, and large numbers of brightly painted canal barges enter the dock. On one bright spring day at the end of Stanley Dock we found a surprisingly small outlet spanned by a narrow bridge. This is the entrance to the vital canal which once so effectively and essentially linked the most important port on the west coast with the equally impressive Hull on the east coast.

How great it is to see so much effort being expended to preserve Liverpool's history, and the accommodation on offer is now good enough to provide a base from which to explore the Mersey estuary and what a friend once described as the 'Scouseland Villages'. Other areas not to be missed at Otterspool, Speke Hall and Hale.

Otterspool is a miracle – it is a three-mile-long promenade area overlooking the now much cleaner waters of the Mersey which has been made from what was once the municipal rubbish dump. A pathway leads back to the Pier Head through an area on which the Liverpool Garden Festival was held in

1984. This event did much to change outsiders' views of the city.

Speke Hall is our favourite half-timbered hall, not because of its obvious beauty but because of its totally unexpected position in the middle of housing and industrial estates surrounded by the only large area of trees on this bank of the Mersey. In days gone by the grounds were subject to flooding and a huge bank of earth was constructed to keep out the overflow. The land between the bank and the river has now been reclaimed and taken over by Speke airport which during the 1990s is set to consolidate its International status. We love standing on the grass bank looking down at the butterflies drinking nectar from the flowers, over the airport runway to the estuary and backwards through an avenue of trees to Speke Hall.

The Norris family built the hall in 1490 when it was eight miles out into the wild country from the tiny but expanding fishing port of Liverpool. The house was a long time in the building and was not complete until 1612, with wings surrounding a central courtyard and an entrance drive crossing a moat by way of a small but most attractive stone bridge. In the courtyard are a couple of ancient yew trees known affectionately as Adam and Eve, whilst inside is a splendid Tudor Great Hall with exquisite plasterwork and walls covered by fine tapestries. The Norris family were faithful Catholics who supported Charles I against Parliament and the Jacobites against the Hanoverians; this accounts for the priest holes in the hall which concealed the catholic clergy who conducted illegal masses for the family, an act punishable by death. The Norris family, however, remained at Speke until 1731 when the supply of male heirs came to an end and it passed through marriage to the Beauclerk family. By 1797 it had been neglected and was in an almost ruinous condition. It was then bought by William Watt, a Liverpool shipping merchant who had the money to lavish on the building. Speke remained with the Watt family until 1921 when the last of the main line, Miss Adelaide Watt, stipulated in her will that it should be held in trust for members of the Norris family and a Mr R.S.F. Hewson. This meant that it could be leased, and it was lived in for a while by F.R. Leyland, another wealthy Liverpool shipowner who entertained the painter Whistler for a time.

Those wishing to know what Liverpool Castle looked like must travel inland to the shores of Rivington Reservoir. Here Lord Leverhulme, who made a fortune from his Sunlight Soap, built a very expensive folly, but unlike with most follies, serious historians should be grateful to the builder.

The most interesting painting in the hall, however, is of John Middleton (1578-1623) who is depicted full size – a staggering nine feet three inches – and who was known as the Child of Hale. Speke Hall is now owned by the National Trust but is leased to Merseyside County Council and is open to the public.

To find the home village of the Child of Hale – some child! – it is best to follow the road towards Widnes and look for a side road down to the riverside. John Middleton was a renowned wrestler and the local landowner Sir Gilbert Ireland actually sent him to London to fight the champion of King James I. The 'child' won and came home with the then substantial prize of £20. The cottage of his birth still stands and he is buried in the churchyard. John is commemmorated in the name of the village inn. To the west of the church is what is left of the Irelands' house whose southern facade was redesigned by John Nash who built Regent's Park terraces in London. From the village a path leads down to the Mersey where next to a cottage stands a disused lighthouse now used as what must be the tallest garden shed in the world!

In the days before Liverpool the area which we now call Merseyside came within the influence of the market town of Ormskirk. Ormskirk's parish church, dedicated to St Peter and St Paul, has both a tower and a spire, a unique feature in the

North of England and often said to be due to the intense
jealousy of two rich sisters one of whom donated the spire, the
other the tower. The truth, however, is far more interesting
than the folklore. On the outskirts of the town at Burscough
are the ruins of an Augustinian Priory founded in 1190. It was
the Canons who were given permission in 1286 to hold the first
official market at Ormskirk. When Henry VIII dissolved the
monasteries between 1536 and 1540 Burscough Priory
suffered badly. Where there was no parish church and the local
folk worshipped at the abbey, the building was retained, but if
a church was available as an alternative, then the monastic
buildings were pulled down. Ormskirk parish church with its
fine spire spelt the doom of Burscough Priory, but pro-
Catholic feeling in the area ran high. Stones were brought to
the church and in 1542 a sturdy tower was constructed to hold
the bell which had once called the brethren to prayer. One of
these bells can still be seen at the back of the church and its
Latin inscription is still legible. The Priory buildings were used
as an unofficial quarry by local farmers and all that now
remains is two pillars, but these are substantial enough to bring
back memories of the days when the old priory church echoed
to the sound of plainsong.

    Although priests of the parish church were appointed by the
Priory between 1190 and 1286 when the first vicar was
appointed, the name Orms-kirk suggests a religious house here
prior to Norman times despite the fact that there is no mention
of it in Domesday. Many experts are of the opinion that some
of the stones in the church are in fact pre-Norman and that
Ormskirk has been a focus for Christian worship for upwards
of a thousand years. Although the church has been much
altered, particularly between 1887 and 1891 when the
architects Paley and Austen undertook a reshaping and
restoration, especially of the nave, many ancient features are
still in evidence. The Derby chapel with its magnificent screen
dates to 1572, and within are two peacefully recumbent figures
impressively carved in alabaster. These may well have come

No one who visited the Garden Festival on the banks of the Mersey in
1984 will ever forget it. For Liverpool it represented a victory for
municipal pride over muck.

from Burscough Priory and are thought to be dated around the late fifteenth century and to commemorate the first Earl of Derby and his two wives. The second figure may well be Lady Margaret, the mother of Henry VII, the founder of the Tudor line, and the grandmother of Henry VIII.

The Derby family had a long, and on the whole friendly, connection with Ormskirk but both the priory which they supported and in particular their majestic, but ill-fated, home at Lathom some three miles to the east of the town have all but vanished. No family and no house suffered so tragically in the Civil War as the Stanleys, the Earls of Derby, and their house, at Lathom. When Henry VII defeated and killed Richard III on Bosworth Field in 1485 the part played by Sir Robert Stanley of Lathom was recognised by the new King who created him the first Earl of Derby. Like his predecessor, the seventh Earl was also a King's man during the 1640s but on this occasion the Derbys had chosen the wrong side, and partly because of this, but mainly because of his part in what became known as the massacre of Bolton, he was sentenced to be returned to that town and there he was beheaded. It was said that his head and body were returned to Ormskirk and buried in separate boxes in the family crypt under the church. This vault is not evident these days and the truth of this bizarre interment cannot be verified. Nor can the precise position of Lathom House which was dismantled following a stubborn siege of the once-magnificent 'medieval castle', and all that remains is the chapel, once part of the estate, which was constructed in 1500. Dedicated to St John the Divine, it is still used regularly for services and is administered from Ormskirk. In the grounds of the chapel is Cromwell's stone which has a couple of holes in it thought to have been used in the moulding of canon balls during the siege of Lathom, when the house under the leadership of Lady Derby bravely resisted the Parliamentary forces. The Lathom grounds are now occupied by the laboratories of Pilkingtons, the St Helens-based glass firm.

Although the influence of its dominant family largely disappeared at the time of the Civil War, Ormskirk's function as a market town continued and in 1800 the population was around 6,000, extensive building taking place as industries based on textiles and iron, and of course farming, developed.

Knowsley Hall, taken around 1940.

Thus a great proportion of the town dates to the Georgian period. The rich soil provided and still provides ideal growing conditions for vegetables and 'Ormskirks' are the favourite potatoes for folk throughout the North West. Despite the removal of many old buildings to make room for car parks a stroll through the traffic-free shopping precinct brings back that old feeling of 'market town nostalgia', a sensation heightened by standing besides what serves for the old market cross and gazing down the street towards the church. Actually 'the market cross' is a clock tower built in 1876 on the site of the old market cross but containing a bell given by Lord Derby in 1684. The reason the Earls of Derby were involved with the market was that the charter passed to the Stanleys when Burscough Priory was dissolved in 1538. They continued to exercise their right, apart from the period following the Civil War and up to the Restoration of Charles II in 1660, until 1876 when the local authority took over.

A look at some of the pub architecture, especially the Buck-ith-Vine on Burscough Street, reminds us of the old coaching days when Ormskirk was a vital staging stop between Liverpool and Preston.

Few small towns can offer more than Ormskirk to visitors, with its fascinating combination of history, folklore, natural history and of course a vibrant and varied market. The most famous of all the market traders was a chap who made pills which one customer described as being 'worth a guinea a box'. The trader's name was Beecham and his little liver pills and a larger-than-life musical son named Thomas have brought world fame to the family. Those who find the hustle and bustle of staying in a city too much may well prefer to base themselves at Ormskirk and from there explore the Scouseland villages.

A narrow road lined by strawberry and potato fields leads to the pretty village of Aughton dominated by the magnificent spire of St Michael's Church. Aughton is mentioned in the Domesday Book and the church rectors are listed from 1246 onwards. Much of the splendid medieval architecture remains, although essential and extensive restoration was carried out in 1914. In the chancel are some exquisite fourteenth-century wooden figures depicting the Stanleys who were also rulers of the Isle of Man. The three legs of Man are clearly shown on the carved heraldic shields carried by the figures. In the churchyard is a sundial dated 1736 and inscribed 'I only count the sunny hours'.

Opposite the church and close to the Stanley Arms is Aughton Old Hall, not open to the public but easily visible from the road. The site has been occupied since Saxon times and the remains of an early fifteenth-century pele tower can be seen in the front garden. The house is reputed to have a 'priest hole' and it is also said that Cromwell used it as his base during his skirmishes around Ormskirk.

Nearby and slicing through an avenue of Scots pines abounding with red squirrels, a bumpy road leads from the National Trust Warden's hut to an extensive system of car parks dovetailing into the sand dunes. Formby Point and Ainsdale National Nature Reserve are linked by a footpath from Freshfield Station and form one of the most extensive dune systems in Britain. Here is one of the last remaining strongholds of the natterjack toad, easily recognised by its running gait and promiment yellow line running down its back. It breeds in the shallow salt pools which also support a variety of plants including such rarities as dune helleborine, round-leaved wintergreen and grass of Parnassus. The drier areas of the dunes are a blaze of colour dominated by evening

An aerial view of Scarisbrick Hall, now a private school for pupils between 4 and 19 years of age. It is a fine example of Pugin's flamboyant architectural style.

primrose, extracts from which are now being used in the treatment of multiple sclerosis. The National Trust area consists of 450 acres of wood and dunelands affording magnificent views seawards over to the Mersey estuary and also to the Lakeland hills and the Isle of Man. Entry is free to pedestrians but there is a modest parking fee. The area is famous for its reserve set aside for red squirrels, but these are not the native British variety with cream-coloured tails but the continental black-tailed sub-species.

In the past Formby village earned its living from fishing and farming. It is said that the first potatoes in England were grown here by men who returned from America with Sir Walter Raleigh. It is now popular as a dormitory for Liverpool and is a place of retirement protected from strong winds by its formidable dunes. St Luke's church is built on the site of a Norman chapel and in the churchyard stands the old market cross made of wood covered in lead which once stood on the village green. The base is hollow and in the days of the plague was filled with vinegar to purify coins left by villagers to pay for food brought by tradesmen who set it down close to the cross.

A tiny hamlet consisting of pub, sixteenth-century corn mill and a church with a lofty and imposing fourteenth-century spire, Sefton retains a medieval tranquillity. The soaring interior of the church is a delight, its ceiling restored by twentieth-century craftsmen whose bosses and moulded beams would not have disgraced the masons who fashioned the sixteenth-century screens and the ornately carved pulpit dated 1635. Fifteenth and sixteenth-century stained glass unearthed recently in the vestry is now incorporated into the windows, and a beautifully preserved display of brasses traces the history of the Molyneux family from the time they arrived in Britain with William of Normandy. The box pews are among the finest in the county and include those occupied by the dog whippers whose job was to exclude unwanted animals from the church and also to control those brought by the congregation to accompany and protect them on the often long walk to and from church. The so called 'Treacle Bible' is a 1595 Miles Coverdale version with some amusing translations which were corrected in the Authorised version of 1611. For example, Jeremiah 8, verse 22 reads, 'There is no more triacle (The Authorised version gives 'balm') in Gilead'. Other curious renderings occur in Psalm 91, verse 5: 'Thou shalt not need to be afraid for any bugges (The Authorised version gives 'terror') by night'. The Molyneux family lived here until they moved to Croxteth and in 1720 their old hall was demolished. Sefton was never really safe from flooding and in the eighteenth century it was decided to regulate the River Alt by diverting its course and ensuring that 5,000 acres of potentially prime farm land did not flood during the winter. There had been a water-powered mill on the banks of the Alt since at least 1590.

Trumpeting elephants, roaring lions, acrobatic monkeys on boots and bonnets of slow-moving cars, real-live zebra crossings and wandering wildebeests make Knowsley Safari Park look and feel like a five-mile tour of the African bush. White Man's Lake, Mizzy Boating Lake and wildlife ponds echo to the calls of exotic and native wildfowl. The sound of the English greenfinch mingles surprisingly well with the snarl of an Indian tiger.

Wild animals are no strangers to Knowsley, since early in the nineteenth century the 13th Earl of Derby, who was a noted zoologist, kept a menagerie of 94 species of mammals and 318 species of birds. Almost 100 acres of his estate was given over to exotic wildlife and 30 attendants were employed to care for them. His extensive library is housed at Knowsley Hall which is not open to the public.

Today's animals are well catered for in the park, which opened in 1971, and visitors are not neglected either. Large car parks, restaurants, souvenir shops, amusement arcades and a fairground ensure that children will enjoy their day out. There is a petrol station so there is no excuse for running out of fuel inside one of the well-fenced wild enclosures. Dogs are not allowed in the wild enclosures but kennels are available.

Following the death of the Earl of Sefton in 1973, his widow gave the delightful Croxteth Hall and its 500-acre estate for public use; this was the biggest-ever gift of land to the city of Liverpool. Merseyside County Council (Museum Departments) have developed Croxteth as a Country Park with a carriage museum, a nature reserve, a walled garden, a display of what life was like in the nineteenth century and a home farm which is loved by children of all ages. There is also a riding school. There are entry fees to some facilities and to the hall itself but access to the park is free. There are good facilities for the disabled.

Straddling a south-west facing ridge overlooking the fertile South Lancashire plain and Skelmersdale New Town is the 304-acre Beacon Country Park which is criss-crossed by a rich tapestry of grassy meadows sheltered by belts of old oak and newly planted conifers. The visitor centre has a shop, a restaurant and a large car park. Footpaths twist and turn from the centre through trees to picnic sites overlooking a golf course. In June the smell of the cut grass mingles with the scent of wild rose and the aromatic mugwort once used, before the discovery of hops, for flavouring ale. Within a mile of the centre is the Beacon Inn and just beyond it on the left is another large car park. A well-trodden path leads from the opposite side of the road to Ashurst's Beacon (often spelt Ashhurst in early documents). This was an invasion beacon forming part of an early warning system for Lancashire stretching from Everton Brow to Lancaster Castle. The views from the Beacon, built by Sir Thomas Ashhurst of nearby Dalton, are spectacular. Blackpool Tower and the Lakeland hills are seen to the north and west, the Mersey and the Welsh mountains to the south-west, the Peaks of Derbyshire to the south-east and the Lancashire Pennines to the north-east.

Below the beacon lie the villages of Parbold and Scarisbrick, both of which lie on the Leeds to Liverpool canal, the latter being an important stop for the miners from the Wigan district on their way to Southport. They completed their journey by means of a connecting coach and horses (see Chapter 2).

Parbold has a brick windmill overlooking the canal, and although now devoid of its sails, it is still in good condition and serving as a rather upmarket clothes shop. A wide variety of colourful pleasure boats moor here or cruise down towards Liverpool via Burscough where the Rufford branch joins the main line at Pinfold Bridge near Scarisbrick. The Red Lion Inn was the miners' rendezvous with the Southport coaches. Scarisbrick Hall was the home of the family of the same name from as early as 1180, and although they were Catholics they managed to play the game of politics very well and kept a firm hold on their estates. In 1814 Thomas Scarisbrick commissioned Foster of Liverpool to rebuild the hall in Gothic style. Thomas died in 1833 whilst the building was still being constructed and his brother Charles and later the surviving sister Anne employed Pugin to bestow even more extravagances on the hall. It is said to be the finest piece of architectural exhibitionism in the country. After a period in the hands of the Marquis de Casteja the hall was sold in 1950 to become a Teachers' Training College, but this was shortlived and it now serves as a private school and is sometimes open to the public during the holidays.

We have spent many happy days cruising between Wigan and the Red Lion watching the rich wildlife on the canal including the colourful kingfisher or enjoying an idle hour or two unsuccessfully fishing. Sometimes if we close our eyes we can almost hear the excited voices of the hard-working Wigan miners and their lasses on their way for a few hours at the seaside. Southport was their resort long before the railway came, and it is to Southport that we turn next.

CHAPTER 2

Southport and the Ribble Estuary

Of all the North Western seaside resorts, Southport has the most to offer the naturalist and has retained most – indeed almost all – of its mid-Victorian gentility. The elegant shopping centre of Lord Street was in fact built into a gap between two sand dunes. It began life not as Southport, but as the village of Churchtown, now relegated to a tiny area of the resort.

The church in question is dedicated to St. Cuthbert. To discover the origins of Christianity in Southport we must go back to the year 687 when St. Cuthbert died on the Holy Island of Lindisfarne, in Northumbria, his remains being interned there in the hope of everlasting peace. Around 200 years later the Danes landed on the island and ransacked the abbey but not before the monks had escaped carrying St. Cuthbert's remains with them. These were valuable since it was believed that they were capable of performing miracles, which could be offered for sale. Before finding a resting place at Durham, the relics were carried around the country for about seven years, and it said that the churches bearing his name mark the places where the bearers rested.

Churchtown may well have had its origins in this way, but its even earlier name was North Meols. The chapel of Mele is mentioned in the Domesday Book, and there are many references in the years which followed, showing how the name gradually changed. It is likely that the derivation is from the Norse *melr* meaning a sand dune. Although the settlement was small, in 1113 there was a thriving fishing community which had to donate a quarter of its catch to the monks of the distant Evesham Abbey. In 1224 Robert de Coudrey granted the right of a market at Melys which was presumably held at the cross near the church. At the dissolution of the abbeys in the 1530s North Meols became a separate parish, and historians have evidence to suggest a community centred around St. Cuthberts – hence Churchtown.

Because it was situated at a crossroads with one track

Southport Pier photographed in 1905.

traversing the sands across the Ribble estuary, the village was of some importance. Thus Churchtown saw more than its fair share of trouble, especially during the Civil War, but by 1730 things had quietened down and in the following ten years St. Cuthbert's was rebuilt but its size indicates that the population was still quite small.

Had it not been for the Victorians' love of sea bathing, Churchtown would have remained an isolated and sleepy village. The sea bathing tradition hereabouts dates back to the year 1219 when St. Cuthbert's Eve was set aside as a fair day. This was on the Sunday following August 20th and it became known as 'Bathing Sunday when folk travelled some distance to tear off their clothes and frolick in the sea'. By the late eighteenth century the event had become rather vulgar and it was found that the most suitable beach was situated about two miles to the south of Churchtown, which was, however, still the only place where visitors could obtain accommodation. A valley flanked by dunes connected the bathing place at South Hawes with the village and the locals transported their guests to and fro by horse and cart. One of the locals named 'Duke Sutton' hit upon the idea of providing accommodation closer to the beach. His first building, more of a hovel than a hotel, was constructed of driftwood in 1792. Around this a settlement grew up and became known as Southport.

The original hotel was built on the Birkdale boundary and so development was only possible to the north and east, and as the marshy area around Churchtown was totally unsuitable for further building, the only suitable land was on the track to Southport. Here we have the origins of Lords Street, still the pride of the modern town. The name arose because it was built on bordering lands of two local Lords of the Manor and the 's' was only dropped around 1830 to give the present name of Lord Street.

As development continued, some of the wet places were drained and the Lords of the Manor insisted that tenants of houses on the eastern side which had been built into the sandhills should continue their gardens across the valley to the roadway. It was these garden areas which the corporation bought and which have transformed Lord Street from an ordinary thoroughfare into a Parisian-looking boulevard. Shops took over the only remaining areas on the westerly side and this street plan remains basically the same to the present day, with straight streets on either side of Lord Street having been built to follow the boundaries of the early house gardens.

There was another vital difference between the growth of Southport and that of the other Lancashire bathing resorts. The Lords of the Manor were absentee landlords. The Heskeths moved to Rossall Hall in 1735, the Bold family lived near Warrington, and the neighbouring Birkdale was owned by the Blundells of Ince Blundell near Liverpool. There was thus no society to be entertained and the Wigan miners and their sweethearts could don their finery and have a carefree day at the seaside, especially on 'Big Bathing Sunday'.

The construction of the Leeds to Liverpool canal in 1770 had brought them to within four miles of the resort, and as explained in the previous chapter, the short trip in a horse and trap was easily organised. The name Southport was not in general use until around 1792 when Doctor Barton christened it by breaking a bottle of champagne in maritime fashion over the hotel. The early driftwood structure was replaced later by a stone building which became known as Dukes Folly as it resulted in Duke Sutton being imprisoned for debt in Lancaster jail in 1803. Although he died in poverty in Churchtown where he had been born, there is no doubt that he laid the foundations of a new town and his folly was eventually let and renamed the South Port Hotel.

Duke Sutton was also a stonemason and he has left examples of his work in St. Cuthbert's churchyard. He earned his nickname of Duke because of a story he told to anyone who would listen. This explained that the Duke of York passed through Churchtown on his way to Scotland.

We spent an exciting day trying to find the precise site of Dukes Folly. The closest point is near the junction of Lord Street and Duke Street at the end of the Boulevard. There, built into the concrete wall at the end of the gardens, are three stone tablets which tell the whole story.

These tablets formed part of a monument which stood from 1860-1912, about 24 yards west of this spot on the site of the Original Hotel or 'Dukes Folly.'

> The year of our Lord 179(7)
> This house was built in memory of D.W. Sutton of North Meols who was the First Founder and Executor of South Port, which was call'd his Folly for many years and it proved that his foresight was his wisdom which should be remembered with gratitude by the Lords of this manor and the Inhabitants of this Place also.
> This column was erected AD 1860 by the Improvement Commissioners as a tribute of respect to the late William Sutton, commonly known as the Old Duke, the Founder of Southport, He was born at Churchtown, North Meols AD 1752 and died there May 22 1840. He erected almost on this spot AD 1792 the First House in what is now the flourishing town of Southport, then a wilderness of sandhills the house originally called 'Dukes Folly' was afterwards known as the Original Hotel. A memorial Tablet, taken from its walls, has been placed on the NE side of this column, and this street has received the name of Duke Street in remembrance of the Old Duke.
> Erected in present setting 1928

Although the Duke lost his money, there is no doubt that he had anticipated the trend which made others rich. From the dawn of the nineteenth century seabathing became more and more popular with the locals but they were eventually swamped by seasonal visitors, doctors recommended not only immersion in seawater but also drinking large volumes of the stuff! Carts took patients out into the tide, and on return the carts rattled with bottles of medicinal seawater to be delivered to those too sick to make the journey to the source. There was a strict code of conduct for bathers which applied at Southport as at other resorts. The rules make amusing reading, so much so that we have a framed copy of the rules on display in our bathroom:

Rules and regulations to be observed on the shore of Southport

1st   There shall be a vacant space of 100 yards between the bathing ground appointed for ladies, and that appointed for gentlemen.

2nd   Any owner of a [bathing] machine going out of the line opposite the front and back posts, to be fined five shillings each time he goes beyond the bounds.

3rd   Any pleasure boat, or other boat, coming within 30 yards of any machine, out of which any person or persons are bathing, the owner of such a boat to be fined five shillings for each offence.

4th   If any fisherman throws out of his boat any entrails of fish, or any dead fish, or leaves them on the shore without burying them in the sand, to be fined five shillings for each offence.

5th   Any person or persons undressing on the beach or in the hills, or crossing the shore naked, within 100 yards from the two outside posts will be dealt with as the law directs for the punishment of such offences.

6th   No person or persons on the charity will be allowed to bathe anywhere betwist the two outside posts on pain of being dismissed.

7th   If any owner of a machine takes any person or persons on the charity within the two outside posts to bathe, he will be fined five shillings for each offence.

> Richard Rimmer, pilot and Richard Ball
> are appointed to see that the above
> rules and regulations are put in force,
> and receive the fines.
> By order of the Lords of the manor,
> John Linaker and Samuel Maddock.
> Stewards.

The fact that these regulations were considered necessary tells us that the society of this time was more permissive than we realise, and an observer writing in 1823 complained at the lack of modesty shown by visitors to Southport. A raising of

In the 1920s car racing was popular on Southport's firm sands. Here we see refuelling going on.

Southport's standards was, however, about to take place.

The railway came to Southport with the 1850 connection to Liverpool, followed five years later by the Manchester link. The town of 'sunsets, spices, sands, spinsters and shrimps' was about to be lifted into the Victorian age. Donkey rides, Punch and Judy shows, organ grinders and monkeys, tea and refreshment rooms, and lodging houses catering for invalids in bathchairs who listened to military bands made Southport a very popular resort. These days Blackpool is the undisputed leading resort of Lancashire's west coast, but initially it was Southport which led the way. In 1871, for example, Blackpool had a population of 6,000 with visitors peaking at around 2,000 whilst the relative figures for Southport were 18,000 and 10,000. In 1880 Southport claimed to be third largest resort in Britain after Brighton and Great Yarmouth, Blackpool lagged behind Southport until its sudden and dramatic surge towards the turn of the present century.

It is as if Southport was overtaken and became trapped in a time warp, producing a sample of Victorian England mothballed for posterity. This is not meant as a criticism, but as a sincere compliment. In its heyday Southport had no difficulty in attracting the very best architects and engineers. For example J. Brunlees, who had just achieved a miracle by constructing a railway across parts of Morecambe Bay to Barrow-in-Furness, was invited to exercise his talents in the construction of a pier to reach the 'distant sea' and thus avoid long donkey trap trips to observe it. He employed railway techniques to sink heavy iron piles into the sand and produced a pier second only in length to that at Southend-on-Sea. A miniature railway still carries passengers to the end of the pier. No less a personage than Paxton, architect of the Crystal Palace, was invited to convert the areas of sand dunes into gardens, and looking at Hesketh Park today, his work seems little less than miraculous. The Southport Flower Show, fortunately saved from extinction in the late 1980s, is famous throughout Britain and helps to retain a tradition established in 1875 with the setting up of the exotically coloured Botanic Gardens.

As the Ribble estuary continued to silt up, the South Port had to find solutions to the problem of the retreating sea. The pier was one answer, and as the nineteenth century drew to its close a marine lake was constructed. Although it was never the prime intention, this lake now attracts more visitors to the resort during the winter as the hobby of birdwatching gathers momentum. During the cooler months of the year, especially during storms, the marine lake offers sanctuary to a varied assortment of seabirds and wildfowl including cormorant, whooper and Bewick swans, scaup, scoter, wigeon, goldeneye, mallard, teal and very occassionally – but excitingly – a long-tailed duck or a flock of pintail.

The sea, however, would not be beaten, silting accelerated, and by 1923 steamers could no longer reach the pier and trips to the Isle of Man, Barrow, Blackpool and North Wales became but a faint memory. Efforts were made to provide alternative entertainment including car racing on the hard flat expanses of sand. Southport began to look inland and the boatman's loss was the gardener's gain. The resort literally bloomed and continued to spend wise money to construct delightful buildings to match the classically styled town hall of 1852. Another gem is the Cambridge Hall opened by Princess Mary

Southport from the air in the early 1950s. In the background you can see Martin Mere before the setting up of the Wildfowl Trust Reserve.

of Cambridge in 1872, but we feel that the 1878 Atkinson Library and Art gallery just fails to work. Trying to combine the glories of the Town Hall and the Cambridge, the Atkinson seems to have fallen between two stools although it is still an impressive building. So too is the School of Science and Art built around 1888 and completing an impressive set of Victoriana now gazed upon by a statue of Victoria herself. We rather think she would be 'amused' to see the town has captured the spirit of her age, the atmosphere of which has also been retained in the Steamport Transport Museum in Derby Road which has both railway engines and vintage road vehicles.

The silting up of the river has provided a varied habitat for wildlife, and three reserves near Southport are of great importance, namely the Ribble Marshes, Martin Mere and Mere Sands.

Visitors travelling along Shore Road between the old villages of Banks and Hesketh Bank near Southport are often thrown into confusion by the total absence of sea. But it was only around a hundred years ago that the tide flowed right up to the road edge. In the intervening period a great area of land has been produced by drainage programmes. This process of reclaiming the estuary of the Ribble has been going on at least since the seventeenth century. The river was canalised as Preston sought to become a major port. In the old days the area must have been overflowing with waders and wildfowl, the populations of which must have been staggering, and the area has long had the reputation of providing protein for the markets of Lancashire. Bird numbers on both the saltmarsh and mudflat are still impressive and in 1979 Banks Marsh was almost absorbed into a huge agricultural complex. Following a well organised outcry by naturalist groups, the Ribble Marshes National Nature Reserve was set up. Banks and Crossens Marshes now form the bulk of the 2182 hectares (5455 acres) of reserve, and a further 120 hectares (300 acres) of Hesketh Out Marsh have been added since then in an agreement with the owners. Management is under the control of the North West (England) region of the Nature Conservancy Council, Blackwell, Bowness-on-Windermere, Cumbria LA 23 3JR.

The only problematical area concerns the anger of many local naturalists who express disaproval of the NCC's agreement with local wildfowlers who are allowed, under licence, to shoot wintering birds, their main quarry being wigeon and pink footed geese. Despite this, however, the NCC point to the fact that wildfowl and wader counts are steadily increasing since the setting up of the reserve.

The reserve is almost equally divided between mudflat and sandbank areas which are ideal feeding areas for waders and what is known locally as greenmarsh which is coloured by a spring carpet of thrift and an autumnal covering of sea aster. This gives both cover and seed and grass food for wildfowl in winter. Visitors are sensibly warned about the dangers of going onto the marsh at high tide, wandering into the muddy gutters or onto the soft mudflats. The greenmarsh is grazed by cattle during the summer.

The marshes are internationally important as huge numbers of waders including dunlin, knot, redshank and bar-tailed godwit gather to feed prior to departing for their breeding grounds in Northern Europe. During the spring the breeding birds return and include around 1500 pairs of common tern, plus an increasing number of Arctic tern and an expanding colony of 10,000 pairs of black-headed gull and as many as 500 pairs of redshank. The nests are so closely packed that the normally solitary redshanks almost appear to breed in colonies here. They also seem to have the good sense to site their nests on high tufts of grass and thus avoid being inundated by the tide. The gulls and terns are not so sensible and in high tides driven by stormy winds, especially after heavy rain, many eggs are destroyed. Until the NCC set up the reserve the grazing summer cattle tended to trample on many nests, but the breeding areas have now been fenced off. Some grazing, however, is essential management policy because without it the grasses would become too tall to be suitable nesting sites for the birds. Nesting species include linnets and one of the most attractive of our summer visitors, the yellow wagtail. The presence of lesser black-backed gulls and herring gulls in recent years has been a problem and they tend to hunt the smaller species. Skylark, meadow pipit, linnet and stonechat also breed, as do mallard and shelduck, the latter two species being encouraged by the beetroot farmer at Old Hollows Farm who has provided an assortment of unusually sited nest boxes among a protective cover of shrubs planted round specially excavated ponds.

Whilst the summer breeding makes the Ribble Marshes important at a national level; it is during the autumn and winter that the area assumes international importance. During autumn almost 100,000 waders pour in from Northern Europe, and although many are on passage to southern Europe and Africa, a large number, probably as many as 30,000, do remain in the area throughout the winter. Knot, dunlin and bar-tailed godwits make up the bulk of the population but there are important numbers of grey plover, oystercatcher and especially redshank. The latter have been carefully monitored over a number of years by students under the leadership of Professor Bill Hale.

Wildfowl populations are also impressive and as many as 30,000 may be on the marsh at any one time between late November and March. Pink-footed geese and wigeon are the most interesting species both to the wildfowler and birdwatcher, but there are also substantial flocks of mallard, teal and pintail, whilst both whooper and Bewick swans also occur.

Birdwatchers visiting the area at times of low tide are never impressed, but on a high spring tide the flocks can be truly spectacular. The best vantage point is close to Crossens when

Martin Mere attracts all those interested in birds, from beginners to experts. Many confined to wheelchairs have become proficient, thanks to the Wildfowl Trust.

the flowing tide pushes oystercatchers, grey plover, curlew and bar-tailed godwits off their feeding grounds and up the river. During August there may be as many as 100,000 knot but as winter sets in the birds move out into Morecambe Bay. Among the more common visitors are redshank and ringed plover, with the occasional rarity such as sanderling, pale as snowflakes, and running like clockwork toys among the mudflats. Spotted redshank, greenshank and whimbrel also occur. Naturally such concentrated flocks attract predators such as the hen harrier, short-eared owl, merlin and the excitingly swift and deadly peregrine.

The *Spartina* grass which has been gradually spreading into the estuary accelerating the silting is something of a mixed blessing. It provides shelter for roosting birds, but also reduces the area of soft open mud which is full of tiny shrimps called *Corophium and Hydrobia,* which are tiny snails, making up the bulk of the diet of such birds as shelduck. The bivalve mollusc *Macoma baltica* or the pink tellin, features in the diet of wader's such as knot, dunlin and redshank which also search for ragworm and lugworm.

High tides between late August and mid-April reveal this site
at its best, but it is always likely to provide interest. There are
good views from the road between Banks and Southport and a
footpath skirts the reserve. It should be realised, however, that
there is some degree of shooting on the reserve between 1st
September and 20th February.

A permit is needed to approach the sanctuary and can be
obtained either from The Warden, Nature Reserve Office, Old
Hollow Farm, Banks, Southport, Merseyside PR9 8DU or from
the Nature Conservancy Council. The reserve is signposted
from Banks village and the footpath along the shoreline is
around seven miles long with access points at Crossens
pumping station and Hundred End. Local farmers often have
cause for complaint as the cars of birdwatchers in search of
rarities block gates into the fields. Old Hollow Farm is
particularly inconvenienced because this is not an official car
park but merely an access point to the NCC office.

Apart from the Ribble estuary there are other spots in the
Southport area which afford exciting birdwatching, including
Martin Mere, and Mere Sands, as well as Ainsdale and Birkdale
and Formby Point which were described in Chapter 1.

The Wildfowl Trust Centre at Martin Mere was established
in 1976 and is well worth the admission fee. Some 353 acres
(142 hectares) offer a refuge for thousands of wintering
wildfowl attracted to the maintained floodlands. There are also
pens in which pinnioned wildfowl are kept for viewing by the
public. An increasing number of hides overlook the stretches of
water, mudbanks and grassy areas. In recent times the
Wildfowl Trust have shown an increasing awareness of other
aspects of natural history with areas set out to encourage the
development of fen plants, and there is now another area set
aside for the display of the increasingly rare natterjack toad.
School parties are encouraged and the reserve appears to be
able to absorb visitors without any interference to the wild bird
populations which are rapidly increasing. Martin Mere, until
drained in the seventeenth and eighteenth centuries to
produce rich farmland, was the largest inland lake in England.
Apparently it was very shallow and a haven for waterfowl, the
descendants of which are those using the Wildfowl Trust's
reserve to this day. Some folk believe that it was into Martin

The packhorse bridge over the River Yarrow at Croston.

Mere that King Arthur's sword Excalibur was tossed after his death.

The reserve is rightly famous for the pink-footed geese which winter in the Southport area, the present population often approaching 20,000 with a high proportion of these

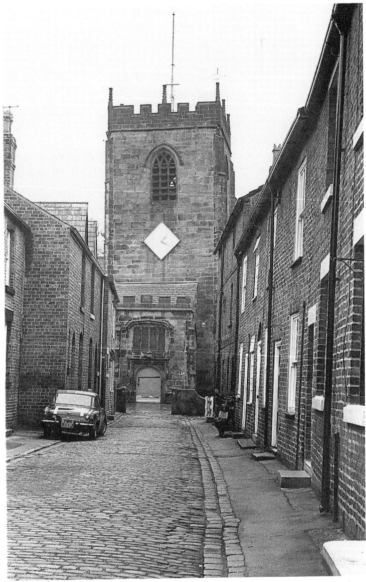

There was, as its name implies, a preaching cross at Croston long before the impressive church was built.

roosting on the reserve. Between November and February the wildfowl counts can be excitingly high with over 1000 mallard and around 3000 teal and pintail regularly recorded along with several hundred wigeon with lesser counts of gadwall shoveler, goldeneye, tufted duck, pochard, goosander, red-breasted merganser and Bewick and whooper swans. Rarities also occur including bittern, water rail, Slavonian grebe, garganey, collared pratincole, marsh and pectoral sandpiper, black and white-winged tern plus lesser yellowlegs. The number of wintering ruff is increasing rapidly and a few hundred now occur regularly each winter. They may well eventually breed in an area which many years ago held many breeding pairs of this attractive wader, along with dunlin, marsh harrier and probably bittern plus black-tailed godwit. Finches are also present in large numbers, doubtless attracted by the grain which the Trust provides for the wildfowl. Corn bunting, greenfinch, goldfinch, redpoll, chaffinch and brambling all occur, and other species also make good use of the free food. Both pheasant and partridge occur regularly, as do collared doves and woodpigeon. With such a variety of potential prey it is not surprising that the sightings of raptors are both regular and varied. The visit of a hen harrier is one of the most exciting sights over the Mere when thousands of anxious birds take to the air with an almost deafening clatter of wings. Other predators include peregrine, merlin, sparrowhawk and short-eared owl, plus one surprising appearance of a hobby.

Whilst many prefer Martin Mere during the colder months of the year, it should nevertheless be regarded as a 'watch for all seasons'. Grasshopper and reed warbler, reed bunting and kingfisher all breed in the area, as do snipe, redshank, coot, moorhen and lapwing. The latter are joined by others coming down from the moorlands plus incomers from more northern areas for the winter when they are joined by curlew and golden plover.

From the A59 Preston to Ormskirk road Martin Mere is signposted from Burscough. After passing along Red Cat Lane and over two bridges, enter the Trust's extensive car park. The complex includes theatre, bookshop, laboratory and snack bar. The reserve is also indicated from the A565 Southport to Preston road, and is open daily, except for Christmas Day.

Mere Sands Wood at Rufford was once an area of commercial sandpits with all the associated disturbance, but it has been rapidly reclaimed by nature since its closure. However, lots of help has been given by the Lancashire Trust for Nature Conservation. Hides have been erected and more are planned, all linked by a network of woodland walks. Because of its geological interest the reserve has been designated a Site of Special Scientific Interest (SSSI).

A variety of woodland species occur here plus some waterfowl frequenting the flooded workings of the old quarry. Little ringed plover have bred here and other interesting species include the common ringed plover, teal, coot, moorhen, little grebe, goldeneye, gadwall, mallard, redshank and snipe. Green and common sandpiper have both been recorded on passage with lapwings and golden plover, which are both regular visitors. Rarities such as bittern and ruddy duck are also worth keeping a keen eye open for.

The woodland has echoed to the notes of blackcap and garden warbler, whilst in winter feeding stations have been set up, which ensures a regular supply of redwing, fieldfare and other members of the thrush family plus redpoll, nuthatch and blue, great, coal and willow tit.

The best approach to the wood is to turn off the A59 Preston to Ormskirk road at the Hesketh Arms and go along the B5246. The reserve is signposted after about 1½ miles you then follow a track to the car park set in the wood. Red squirrels occur here. The Trust's Information Centre is sited close to one of the hides and overlooking the flooded workings of the old quarry. It is open on most days of the year.

The historian is also well provided for in this area, and we love to visit Rufford Old Hall and view the historic Carr House which is privately owned.

Close to the banks of a branch of the Leeds to Liverpool Canal and the River Douglas, which is a tributary of the Ribble, stands the fine old half-timbered Rufford Old Hall. Now administered by the National Trust, the hall was originally constructed for Sir Thomas Hesketh who controlled this area between 1416 and 1458. As with any such building, there have been many alterations since, but the Great Hall with its hammerbeam roof must have witnessed many an historic event.

In the 1580s, for example, it is highly likely that the actor named William Shakeshaft (*alias* William Shakespeare) performed for the influential Hesketh family. Around 1760 the Heskeths moved to their New Hall, and after a period of decline the Old Hall was taken over by the National Trust in 1936. It is well worth the entrance fee and is open during the summer months except on Fridays. The collections of tapestries, oak furniture, pictures and ancient weapons are of national as well as local interest, whilst for those interested in country life the Philip Ashcroft collection of local artefacts donated to the Trust in 1946 is well worth detailed exploration. Whatever the weather, Rufford has much to offer and there are woodland walks alongside the canal which is much favoured by local anglers.

Situated on the old Preston to Liverpool turnpike, the villages of Tarleton, Bretherton, Much and Little Hoole have now been mainly bypassed by the new road. In 1988 conservationists were appalled by the demolition of the old toll house which stood on the junction of the roads between Preston, Liverpool and Southport. Some other historic buildings have been left alone, including the Ram's Head Inn and Carr House. The Ram's Head, originally built in 1640, did great service during the nineteenth century as a coaching inn, and evidence of its former use can still be seen despite an updating which included the construction of a night club. The old stables remain, as do the beamed ceilings.

Nearby is Carr House which was built in the early seventeenth century by Thomas and Andrew Stones for their brother John who was a sheep farmer. The family fortune depended upon the international trade in wool. The faded inscription above the door reads 'Thomas Stones of London, Haberdasher and Andrew Stones, of Amsterdam, merchant, in 1613.' The house is of great interest to scientists because it was here that Jeremiah Horrocks, a young curate of Hoole Church who lodged there, made history on Sunday November 24th 1639. He predicted that on that day the planet Venus would pass between the earth and the sun – a transit never before observed. Luck was with the young man as early evening mist suddenly cleared and allowed a clear sighting of the event that his mathematical genius had enabled him to predict. Horrocks died suddenly in 1640 at the age of 23, but his contribution to science was such that there is a memorial plaque to him in Westminster Abbey.

Carr House, a fine example of Jacobean architecture, was in a sad state of repair until the 1960s when the late Barry Elder restored it to house his famous collection of dolls. This has now been transferred to the Judges' Lodgings Museum in Lancaster (see Chapter 5), and the house, now privately owned, has been expertly and tastefully renovated.

Nearby and still on the busy 'new' road is Tarleton's 'old' church which is one of the finest buildings in the North West. St. Mary's dates to 1719 and is brick-built apart from the belfry which is of beautifully cut stone. Replaced by a larger church in 1886, the old building, constructed by the Lord of the Manor, became redundant. There is a notice by the porch, however, which tells us that its fabric is still maintained by the Redundant Churches Fund administered from the unusually named St. Andrew by-the-Wardrobe Church on Queen Victoria Street, London. The cemetery is still used and kept wonderfully well, but the church itself is sensibly kept locked. It is easily possible, however, to peep through the window and see the old oil lamps still hanging and the splendid gallery reached by a staircase.

The overall impression we have of these villages is that, despite the proximity of a modern road, tranquility is still easily found. Nowhere is this more evident than at Much Hoole, dominated by its impressive seventeenth-century church. Here it was that Jeremiah Horrocks conducted his short working life. In the days before folk learned to manage rivers and to control water levels these villages fought a constant battle against floods. The area was controlled from the large parish church at Croston, one of the most unspoiled large villages in the county.

Stone and brick-built cottages line one side of the main street, and on the other side the River Yarrow meanders around high stone banks constructed to prevent flooding. The river is crossed by an ancient packhorse bridge dating to at least 1682. The village centre is dominated by a church of cathedral-like proportions dedicated to St. Michael, with records dating back to the eleventh century. Here, whilst making a radio programme on village churches, the churchwarden Bob Bretherton taught us – or rather tried to teach us – to ring bells. St. Michael's is approached along a narrow street of small brick cottages at the entrance to which is a cross from which Croston (the town of the cross) derives its name. There was probably a wayside cross here in the seventh century around which Christians gathered and looked down on the then marshland and Martin Mere. The old cross has long been lost, but the present one, although only dating to 1950, has already blended well with the village scene.

Next to the church is a school founded in 1372 by John of Gaunt who virtually governed England on behalf of the boy King Richard II. In 1660 the Puritan James Hyett, who was the vicar of Croston, provided the church with a handsome endowment, but the days of the Puritans were numbered as Charles II returned to England, and in 1662 Hyett lost his position. This was because he bravely refused to obey the Act of Uniformity by declining to use the Anglican prayer book. He died in Preston in 1663 and is remembered in Croston by a stone plaque on the school wall.

Croston also has a fine old rectory and a set of almshouses built in 1802 to commemorate the jubilee of King George III and paid for by the Masters family who dominated the village for many centuries in the joint roles of priest and landowner. Anyone wanting to understand the history and natural history of this low-lying land should spend time at Croston which dominated the area for so long. The Fylde is a similar area on the opposite side of the River Ribble. As there is no bridge over the Ribble until Preston, Southport and the Fylde have been more isolated than one would imagine, and have developed differing characteristics.

CHAPTER 3

Blackpool and the Fylde

Our introduction to the Fylde was in the late 1940s, when we journeyed from Cumbria (then Furness in Lancashire) during the school holidays to help an uncle who had a garage on the main road from Preston into Blackpool. It was hard work pumping petrol up into a glass measure on the top of the pump and then opening a valve to allow the fuel to run down by gravity into the tank of the car. Our reward was to be taken on exploratory trips around the Fylde in a pre-war Jaguar which roared like a tiger, plus the occasional paid-for evening at one of the theatres or dancing at the Tower ballroom.

The Fylde is a fascinating combination of ancient and modern, and those in search of the early history of the area should perhaps begin at Kirkham but should not forget Lytham, once an important port on the Ribble estuary.

Visitors approaching Kirkham from Wrea Green are following the line of the Roman road which is now buried beneath the modern town. The road is known in parts as Danes Pad and probably indicates that the Roman road was still in use for a number of centuries after the departure of the legions. Their road connected Ribchester to the old port of *Portus Setantiorum*, probably off Fleetwood and now swallowed up by sand deposited by centuries of erosive action of the Irish Sea (see Chapter 4). Kirkham's Roman fort is now buried beneath a complex of modern housing.

The settlement had its church (Scandinavian Ciric-ham meaning church village) prior to the Norman conquest and from 1287 had its charter for a market and fair by decree of Edward I. The area around was governed from Kirkham by 'thirty sworn men'. In 1296 Kirkham was allowed by the powerful Abbot of Vale Royal in Cheshire to call itself a Borough. When Henry VIII dissolved the Abbeys, the advowson of Kirkham was given to the Dean and Chapter of Christ Church, Oxford. There is still a heavy volume of traffic flowing through despite the close proximity of modern

Although this garage was at the toll booth near Lancaster its design was similar to the pumps we used to fuel holidaymakers' vehicles outside Blackpool in the 1940s.

bypasses, but the steep main street is a shopper's joy. Old shop fronts display modern wares, especially during the Thursday market when farmers rub shoulders with housewives and visitors and old folk have a good gossip. The focal point is the cobbled square with its fine example of fish stones where the freshwater and sea fish were laid out for the inspection of prospective buyers. Modern hygiene prevents such practices, but those of us with good imaginations can still conjure up the smells and sounds of fish being filleted on these stones. It is rather a pity that some unwise development in the old market area has destroyed some of the atmosphere, but Kirkham is not the first market town to suffer at the hands of developers. Round about is an impressive collection of Georgian buildings and inns indicating the importance of the town during the age of coaching when Kirkham was a halt between Preston and the Fylde coast. A particularly impressive house opposite the fish stones is now used as a doctor's surgery.

Lytham Windmill and Green about 1947.

It is rather unusual in the context of ancient towns to find the parish church tucked away along a back street. St. Michael's was rebuilt in 1822 at a then substantial cost of £5000 with a 150-feet high steeple added around 1843 whilst the chancel was redesigned in 1853. Within the church are a number of interesting artefacts from earlier churches including a Clifton family memorial which records the passing of

A virgin masculine
Whom sacred love did much refine
In foreign schools assiduous
And free his soul from faulty ignorance.

There is also a monument to Sir Thomas Clifton of Lytham dated 1688. A decorated tomb of the family is sited on the south wall. The Cliftons were a powerful family based at Lytham who remained stoutly, and often tragically, devoted to the Catholic cause during the seventeenth century. Hanging in the nave is a magnificent two-tier brass chandelier made by Browns of Wigan and dated 1725.

Leaving the church and returning to the main road, we pass the National School established in 1814. A left turn follows Preston Street, known locally as Hill Street, to one of the town's old windmills which has been impressively restored and is now a white-painted residence of considerable charm renamed Winde Milne. The mill has not worked since the early 1900s and was described as derelict in the 1950s. How grand it is to see such an important part of a town's history saved from destruction. Returning to the centre down Hill Street brings us to the Black Horse, a fine old coaching inn with a sweeping archway through which many a weary and chilled traveller must have passed looking forward to a hot meal and a warm bed. The houses lining the street are a fascinating mixture of old cottages and early eighteenth-century Georgian residences. Some of the cottages have weaving cellars, an indication of the trade on which Kirkham once depended. During the eighteenth century Kirkham was an important flax-producing town, with three families dominating the trade. These were the Langtons, the Shepherds and the Birleys, the latter giving some fine stained glass to the church. Their imposing residence, Hillside House, situated opposite the Black Horse Hotel, was constructed in the 1820s. Its iron-railed outer staircase, fanlighted doorway and handmade bricks laid in Flemish bond ensure that this building attracts all who love Georgian domestic architecture. The Langton family lived in Ash House, built in the eighteenth century on Church Street. This is now the DHSS office. An even older dwelling dated 1729 is No 14 Preston Street over the door of which are the initials HIE.

Many such examples remain, but alas many others along with the flax mills have gone, but a stroll along Mill Street and a glance at the names of the side streets will take one back to times when Kirkham tried hard to establish itself as a centre of commerce. The flax was imported mainly from the Baltic into a major port on the east bank of the River Wyre sited at Wardleys near to Poulton-le-Fylde.

Flax is also known as Linum and belongs to the Linaceae genus of plants which have long narrow leaves bearing flowers along the stem. The fibres are pulped to make flax (linen), whilst the seeds are crushed to produce linseed oil. Ropes were also made from flax and Kirkham lived in peace and prosperity for almost 200 years. When the railway came to the Fylde in the 1840s, it passed through the tiny suburb of Wesham. Industry attracted big business to Wesham and soon a line of buildings connected the one-time hamlet to Kirkham. The

Wreck of the *Mexico* on the Southport shore. The Southport and St. Annes-on-the-Sea lifeboats were wrecked and both crews lost in going to the rescue, 10th december, 1886.

Fylde, however, is distant from the big city financiers and the boom times have now gone, Kirkham has now – some would say happily – reverted to its original function as the Fylde's major market town. It certainly has the historical pedigree and central position to warrant this role.

A major port of the Fylde and the home of the Clifton family was at Lytham, which is an ideal place from which to begin an exploration of the coastline.

In recent years Lytham St Annes has been fighting an almost constant battle to avoid being amalgamated with Blackpool, which is a shame since Lytham and St Annes had only themselves been amalgamated as a borough in 1922. Lytham is by far the oldest settlement with its origins established before the Norman Conquest and was referred to in the Domesday Book as Lidum. The focus for Lytham's history is the late Georgian mansion of Lytham Hall, ancestral home of the Clifton family. This is sited on what was a monastic farm owned by the monks of Durham, with the thirteenth-century church dedicated to St. Cuthbert who also, as we have seen, had associations with Durham. It was rebuilt in 1770 and again in 1834, reflecting the increasing size of population and affluence. Lytham earned its living from fishing and also from

Bathing in 1910 was more of a fashion parade than good exercise. Anyone trying to swim very far in these outfits would soon become waterlogged.

St. Annes Pier around 1900.

ship building which continued until the early 1940s when parts of the Mulberry floating harbours were constructed here in deadly secret and in preparation for the allied invasion of Normandy. The last vessel to be built at Lytham was the Windermere Car Ferry completed in 1955.

At the eastern end of the seafront is a large and accurately restored windmill overlooking Lytham Green. The flat land of the Fylde is true windmill country and this example built in 1805 on the site of a previous mill was damaged in 1929 when a freak gust of wind set the wheels spinning the opposite way, damaging the machinery and ending the mill's working life. There is plenty of parking near the mill and there are seats overlooking the beach which are used by the holidaymakers in the summer and by birdwatchers in winter. The same dual function is fulfilled by Fairhaven Lake which is used for yachting, motor boating and rowing in the season and is also another haven in winter much favoured by wildfowl. Lowther Gardens situated close to the West Beach has colourful flower beds plus tennis courts, putting and bowling greens plus an indoor swimming pool now considered essential in these northern climes. To the east of the town serious sportsmen are catered for and there are splendid golf courses including Royal

It is thought that the Evening Primrose was brought to Britain from North America in the ballast of ships carrying cotton. The Red Indians used its oil to heal wounds and stiff joints, and it has been used by modern doctors in the treatment of muscular dystrophy, some forms of breast cancer, and for pre-menstrual tension.

Lytham which sometimes hosts the British Open.

St. Annes was the scene of the worst lifeboat disaster in British history. In 1886 the crew answered a distress signal from the German barque, *Mexico*. All thirteen men of the St Annes crew were lost plus all but two of the Southport lifeboat. Some good did come of the tragedy for it led to improvements in lifeboat design. The memorial to the crews is in St. Annes Alpine Gardens.

St. Annes developed in response to the tourist boom of the nineteenth century as seabathing became popular. It was meant to be, and in fact still is, a genteel alternative to Blackpool. St. Annes pier is a delight first built in mock Tudor style in 1855 but with the entrance built just after 1900. Some damage was sustained to the end of the pier in 1974 and the theatre was destroyed. The resort is typified by red-brick Victorian mansions which were used by businessmen who commuted to their town businesses via the developing railway network. Private hotels also catered for visitors who came to enjoy the spectacular sport of sand-yacht racing which is still popular. The idea of the town called on the brains of one man and the brass of another, an irresistible combination. Thomas Fair was the agent of the Clifton family and had expressed the opinion that the dunes were ripe for development. In 1874 Elijah Hargreaves visited the area and the two decided to name the new resort after the chapel of ease built in 1873 and dedicated to St. Anne. Most of the essential money came from Hargreaves mill-owning friends from the industrial belt around Haslingden and along the Rossendale Valley.

The pier at St. Annes is in need of some renovation but the promenade gardens are spruce and the boating lake is still popular as are the miniature railway and the heated open-air swimming pool. There is also an impressive indoor pool. Remnants of a bygone age are seen in the form of bathing huts close to the safe beach and in winter birdwatchers use the huts as shelter whilst watching the waders feeding on the sand and mud banks. Before describing Blackpool, some attention should be given to the wildlife of the area.

A seaside resort as important and as heavily populated as Blackpool can hardly be expected to offer excitement to experienced and demanding bird watchers. But first impressions are often wrong, and in 150 years or so the rich wildlife which once dominated the low-lying area has shown remarkable resilience. Although much building has taken

However wet and windy the weather, Blackpool's Golden Mile was heaven to the Lancashire textile workers. Even a gale-force wind would have been quiet after the clatter of the looms.

place, oases for wildlife are still present even during the peak of the holiday season. All the naturalist has to do is to get up early while the previous night's revellers are still sleeping.

The long stretch of coast beginning at Lytham and Fairhaven Lake and ending at Squires Gate offers four separate habitats. The lake is a haven for wildfowl, the sand dunes are extensive and the beach at low tide provides exellent watching for those

Blackpool's defences are normally able to withstand high seas and strong winds.

keen on waders and gulls, but once the tide is in, then sea watches can be equally rewarding. The variety of coastal flowers is impressive and includes sea radish, lady's bedstraw, rest harrow, evening primrose, biting stonecrop, haresfoot trefoil, yellow rattle, hearts-ease pansy, harebell, common storksbill and lesser burdock. On the beach a variety of shells bears witness to the rich supply of food available to birds. In the muddy areas the U-shaped burrows of lugworm seem to be everywhere with a depression at the head end and a coil of defecated sand at the other. Lugworm and ragworm provide abundant food for waders.

The value of Fairhaven Lake speaks for itself, but an added attraction is the surrounding belt of vegetation including hazel and alder plus sea buckthorn whose orange berries provide food for autumn migrants. Below the lake and the walled promenade are areas of shingle which are always worth examining closely in search of perfectly camouflaged birds, particularly ringed plover. The Lake itself can be relied upon to provide an interesting variety of birds including Canada and greylag geese plus a weird assortment of 'farmyard mallards',

'Natural' mallards, tufted duck, scaup, goldeneye and wigeon are all regular, as are cormorant, red-breasted merganser and heron, but there are occasional bursts of excitement including the sighting of red-necked and grey phalarope which were present at the same time! The melodious warbler which turned up in August also caused a stir. A black-throated thrush and a black redstart have been recorded in November, and a black-eared wheatear has been recorded in April.

Waders seen over the wall include redshank, black and bar-tailed godwit and curlew; impressive flocks of sanderling, dunlin, ruff, knot, oystercatcher and ringed plover build up to impressive numbers, especially during the first three months of the year. Grey plover also turn up in small numbers. On a flowing tide driven in by a high wind the wall can provide welcome shelter for the watcher, as can the many shelters which are provided for the use of summer holidaymakers. Springtime visitors can be entertained by watching house martins gather mud to build their cup-shaped nests.

The vegetation around the lake provide nest sites for stonechat, reed bunting, common whitethroat, linnet, greenfinch, chaffinch and the occasional yellowhammer. In autumn the buckthorn berries are appreciated by the thrush family, particularly fieldfares, and wood pigeons also feed greedily upon them. These species are also found in the dunes where they are joined by the odd pair of oystercatcher and ringed plover which seek out areas of shingle in sheltered spots between the sandhills held together by extensive growths of marram grass.

The marram can also provide the sea-watcher with protection and a spot to prop up the essential tripod holding the telescope. Those with patience will no doubt add to the already notable list which includes cormorant, common, arctic, little and sandwich terns (from March to September), red-throated, and great northern diver (winter), plus puffin, guillemot, razorbill, great-creasted and red-necked grebe, gannet plus manx shearwater (regular) and sooty shearwater (rarely). Common scoter (over 1000 often seen in January and February) are seen regularly in winter with the occasional velvet scoter rewarding the diligent watcher, plus regular sightings of wigeon, pintail, shelduck and occasionally a long-

View of Blackpool Promenade in the busy days just after the Second World War.

tailed duck or an eider. Gulls are obviously regular, as is the fulmar, but every bird should be examined, especially in winter when Mediterranean gull may occur, and in spring when flocks of up to 20 little gulls may well turn up plus glaucous and Iceland gulls in winter. Skuas and kittiwakes can also be expected from November to April and a long scan over the waves in autumn may reveal passing storm and Leach's petrel.

As the tide ebbs, the strand line should be examined as rock pipit, snow and Lapland bunting plus shore lark can be expected.

Fairhaven Lake is signposted off the A584 coast road from Lytham to Blackpool. There is parking by the lakeside and also access to the dunes and shore by parking on Fairlawn Road. Although it involves a long walk, we prefer to park at Fairhaven and proceed to Squires Gate along the beach, returning through the dunes. Two comparatively minor sites which could be combined with the visit to Fairhaven are Lytham Gardens and Lytham Hall Park. The former has been visited by a firecrest in November and a yellow-browed warbler during October. In Lytham Hall Park all three species of woodpecker have been recorded, as have lesser whitethroat and hawfinch, neither species being at all common in this area.

All this proves that it is possible to enjoy excellent bird watching around Blackpool, but this certainly has little to do with what the normal visitor to the resort has in mind. B stands for Blackpool and Brashness, with the resort acting as the working man's sea-air lung. It developed as a colourful ribbon of vibrant life divided into sections by three piers and overlooked by the girdered steel finger of the Tower with its 518-foot (158 metre) summit providing stunning views of the throngs looking like ants below. Blackpool may have started late but it developed much more quickly than most resorts. In 1840 it was a village, yet by the turn of the century it attracted three million visitors each year. By 1960 this figure had soared to more than eight million, arriving at first by train and gradually by coach and private car. Our work in the summers of the 1950s at Warburtons Clock Garage on the edge of the resort told us clearly enough that the boom was on as we filled the tanks of Austin A35s and 40s, Morris Minors, Jowett Javelins, Triumph Mayflowers, Hillman Minx, Sunbeam

Blackpool taken from the North Pier around 1900.

Talbots, Vauxhall Velox and a host of other makes now part of our motoring history. But the annual summer airlift to the Spanish resorts slowed the rush to the North Western coast as the Wakes weeks faithful sought guaranteed sun and cheap drink. Blackpool's short history, however, has always demonstrated the resort's resilience and this is still very obvious in the 1990s.

The railway reached Blackpool's single row of seafront cottages in 1846; the Central Station and North Pier opened in 1863; in 1876 the Winter Gardens threw wide its doors and from this time onwards Blackpool was in full swing in its pursuit of tourists. The visitor was all-powerful, and whatever was wanted, the resort would provide. The Tower came in 1894 and provided a circus (recently closed), a ballroom, aquarium, a heritage exhibition and a number of bars and restaurants. The Tower had class, in complete contrast to the Golden Mile which spread out below it. Actually the Golden Mile infringes the Trades Description Act as it is not much more than a quarter of a mile in length, but its showmen never sold visitors short if all they wanted was spectacle and they didn't mind being relieved of their hard-earned cash. We miss the fortune tellers, the freak shows and the cheap jacks who have been replaced by discos, bingo and bars which sound and look just like similar establishments anywhere in the world.

One thing has not changed – Blackpool still has the very best

The Market Place with St Chad's Church in the background taken about 1895.

of summer variety. There are three piers, each with its own theatre offering the full spectrum of what Lancastrians call 'turns' to please children, pop-mad teenagers and nostalgic grannies. Thora Hird once told us that no up-and-coming star could afford to turn down a season at Blackpool, and things haven't changed.

The philosophy behind the Pleasure Beach hasn't changed either and the aim is to frighten visitors but ensure that all the rides are completely safe – or almost so. 'Accidents here are as rare as hen's teeth', we were once told and the safety record bears out this confidence. The Pleasure Beach was founded by W. G. Bean in 1890 and his aim 'To found an American-style amusement park where adults could feel like children again.' The complex was taken over on Bean's death by his son-in-law L.D. Thompson; this family still control events and in 1989 commissioned Lord Lichfield to produce a photographic portrait of the Pleasure Beach. The rides are a mixture of modern and traditional, including Sir Hiram Maxim's Flying Machine which was opened in 1904 and is still popular. The Grand National and the Big Dipper have to be experienced to be believed but we both prefer to stand and watch, and listen to the screams of the riders whilst struggling ourselves with some sticky candy floss.

Whatever your holiday demands may be, Blackpool and the Fylde can almost certainly meet them. There is both roller and ice skating, Stanley Park is one of the best in the country with nearby golf courses and a model village, the zoo is better than average and its animals are well looked after. The season has been extended by the illuminations which light up the resort from September to the end of October. Once the lights have gone out, the beaches are taken over for the winter by the birds, as is also the case with Marton Mere.

Surrounded by a large commercial caravan park, Marton Mere, set in a hollow left behind after the Ice Age, is 10 acres (4 hectares) of water fringed by reeds. The reed beds have been substantially reduced due to the commercial pressures of being a prime site close to a holiday resort, but they are nevertheless still impressive once the holidaymakers have departed.

Over 160 species have been recorded at Marton Mere, over 30 of which breed despite the setting, and this must make it, acre for acre, one of the most impressive bird sites in Lancashire. Visiting winter wildfowl include Bewick, whooper and mute swan, pink-footed and white-fronted goose, mallard, scoter, scaup, smew, long-tailed duck, pochard, wigeon, ruddy duck, tufted duck, gadwall and goosander, and the very rare garganey has been recorded in summer. Waders seen include whimbrel (in spring), curlew, redshank, spotted redshank, Temminck's stint, little stint, dotterel and collared pratincole (spring), common and curlew sandpiper plus both common and jack snipe. Other species include both bittern and little bittern, red-necked phalarope, little and spotted crake (the former in spring, the latter in autumn), water rail, bearded tit, black-necked grebe, Mediterranean and little gull, short-eared owl, marsh and hen harrier plus peregrine and hobby. Songbirds recorded include Lapland and ortolan bunting, reed bunting, reed and sedge warbler, rock pipit, stonechat, whinchat, skylark, meadow pipit and linnet.

The corporation refuse tip is sited nearby, but is discreetly screened and attracts a variety of gulls including all the

The Old Fire Station at Singleton.

common species plus wintering glaucous, Iceland and greater black-backed gulls.

The best way to find Marton Mere is from the M55 motorway following the signs for Blackpool until you reach the Clifton Arms. Marton Mere can be reached by turning right, and there is also access from Stanley Park via Great Staining. From Marton Mere a stream called Main Dyke runs out to Poulton-le-Fylde and empties into the Wyre at Skippool.

Reading the history of Poulton-le-Fylde, it is easy to understand why the townsfolk consider Blackpool to be something of an upstart. After the Norman Conquest the Poulton area was given by the Conqueror to Roger de Poitou who in turn granted it in 1094 to the Priory of St Mary in Lancaster. The Church of St. Chad is a delightful building looking at its best in March when it is surrounded by masses of crocuses. There has been a church on this site since Norman times, and probably even before this as it is dedicated to St. Chad, a seventh-century Northumbrian missionary. The Venerable Bede in his *Ecclesiastical History of the English Nation* tells that 'Chad was consecrated bishop and immediately devoted himself to the task of keeping the church in truth and purity, to the practice of humility and temperance and to study. He visited cities and country districts, towns, houses and strongholds, preaching the gospels, travelling not on horseback but on foot after the apostolic example'.

The oldest part of the present church is early seventeenth century, the rest being mainly Georgian. The interior is true Georgian with a gallery running around three sides and with a magnificent staircase, a most unusual feature in churches. There is a Jacobean pulpit, a seventeenth-century screen in the baptistry and impressive memorials to the Fleetwood-Hesketh family, including wall monuments and a vault dated 1699. The church overlooks the pedestrianised market square, and at the opposite end are signs of less peaceful times. Here are the stocks and the whipping post as well as the stone fish slabs. The stocks were erected in 1351, and these and the whipping post were all in use until well into the nineteenth century.

Poulton had a rail link before Blackpool, and early tourists disembarked here and travelled the remaining four miles to the developing Golden Mile by horse and trap. When the railway reached Blackpool in 1846, this episode in Poulton's life came to an end. It has, however, found another niche in recent years, and sensitive house construction has enabled the town to become a popular dormitory area close enough to the M55 to attract workers from Manchester and Liverpool. The same applies, although to a lesser degree, to the Fylde villages of Singleton, Woodplumpton and Freckleton.

At the entrance to Singleton stands the Miller Arms, which commemorates the wealthy family whose fortune was made from the cotton mills of Preston during the nineteenth century. They lived in Singleton Hall, not open to the public and tucked away out of sight, but the impressive gates stand just beyond the post office. On the corner of Church Road there is a striking black and white building with red doors above which are carved the words 'Fire Engine'. Although it now serves as an electricity sub-station, it is easy to imagine the horse-drawn appliance thundering out of the gates and along the narrow main street lined with neat cottages each with its colourful garden. At the top of Church Road, fringed by maturing trees, is St. Anne's Church, built in 1860 by Thomas Miller on the site of an earlier building. In the sanctuary is a black oak chair inscribed 'John Milton, author of Paradise Lost and Paradise

Meg Shelton's Church at Woodplumpton. Note the influence of Sir Christopher Wren on the design of the bell tower.

Regained 1671'. The lych gate of the old church still stands on the opposite side of the road.

Too often we ignored the signs to Woodplumpton whilst on our way to Blackpool, but when we finally made a detour to the village we found it a fascinating throwback to life in Old England, centred around the church. Outside is a set of well-preserved stocks behind which is a mounting block, a relic of the time when horses were the main transport. This, and the church of St. Anne, are listed as historic monuments. Close examination of the stocks reveals an inscription of AB, probably the maker's initials, and the number 73 indicating the year, but not the century. We would guess the date to be 1773, and there is a set of pillars from even older stocks set into the smaller of the two entrance gates to the church. The main entrance is through an impressive lych gate. A feature of the churchyard is a huge boulder which is said to mark the last resting place of Margaret Hilton – better known as Meg the Witch! Locally she had been known as Meg Shelton.

It was said she entered into a wager with the Haydock family who had a cottage at nearby Catforth in which Meg used to live. The family wagered that she could not turn into a hare and outrun the family dogs. She did, however, exclude one black dog. But the family cheated and the black dog almost caught the hare, biting its back legs as the race was almost won. It is said that Meg got her cottage, but limped badly from this time onwards and was always in a foul temper. She was accused of laming cattle, stealing milk and causing the remainder to go sour. When she died, apparently crushed between a water barrel and a well, she was buried at Woodplumpton, but her body kept rising to the surface! She was finally kept in place by being re-buried face downwards with a huge boulder rolled over the grave. Whatever the truth of the matter, a Margery Hilton of Catforth was buried in the churchyard on May 2nd 1706. And there is also a huge boulder over her grave which nobody feels like moving!

The word Plunton appears in the Domesday Book and a church may have been sited here in the days of the Saxon Earl Tostig. There was certainly a church here in 1552, and some local historians have suggested a date of between 1509 and 1549. The present tower, however, was completed in 1748 and its octagonal cupola-like shape suggests that the architect had studied the work of Sir Christopher Wren. The clock set into the tower is dated 1747, suggesting that the new tower was provided with a more up-to-date timepiece than the sundial on the old tower. This bears the date 1637 and is now sited in the churchyard, although there is another possibly older sundial actually incorporated into the tower. The church looks at its best in the morning sun when it seems that even Meg Hilton is at peace!

Another of the Old Fylde villages is Freckleton which was listed in the Domesday Book under the name Frecheltun which derives from the Anglo-Saxon meaning 'an enclosed area'. Freckleton is now a long straggling village stretching along the north bank of the Ribble. The brick-built church dates to 1837 and has box pews and an eight-sided Jacobean pulpit ornately carved and bearing the inscription 'Cry aloud, spare not: lift up thy voice like a trumpet', which came originally from the church at Kirkham. Until the flood plain of the Ribble was tamed by canalising the river, much of the land around Freckleton was marshy, and at Halfpenny Bridge there is an old toll house, now isolated, but from it the line of the old turnpike road, now grassed over, can be seen heading straight across the marshes to old Freckleton.

Nowhere does the old name of Fylde seem more appropriate than here, as it derives from the Anglo-Saxon 'gefilde' meaning level green fields. This describes very well the land sandwiched between the Ribble and the Wyre, and it is to the latter river that we now turn our attention.

CHAPTER 4

Fleetwood and the River Wyre

Many visitors to Fleetwood gazing across to Knott End know that this is the estuary of the River Wyre, but do not know where the river rises or anything very much about its fascinating history. We often make the 50-mile journey to the Trough of Bowland, which is the source of the Wyre. The Trough is a soaring pass climbing steeply to a height of just over 1000 feet (305 metres) from Dunsop Bridge, which was in Yorkshire before the county boundaries were redrawn in 1974, to the Lancashire village of Abbeystead. Now both villages belong to the Red Rose county and the old boundary stone at the summit of the Trough serves no geographical purpose, but it is still a vitally important historical landmark. We love to stand at the stone and watch a skylark ascend silently from Old Yorkshire only to tumble down in a flurry of song and feathers to its nest in a tussock of Lancashire grass.

Up on these breezy uplands rise two of the most beautiful rivers in Britain – the Hodder which feeds the Ribble and, on the opposite side, the Wyre.

As is the case with many rivers, the precise source of the Wyre is difficult to place and in fact it has two sources called the Marshaw and the Tarnbrook. It is the Marshaw Wyre which rises among the sphagnum moss close to the boundary stone. In the days before bandages, sphagnum was known as 'battle grass'. If you squeeze it, water comes out of it as from a heavy sponge. It was therefore dried and pressed onto as well as into wounds, its efficiency helped by the presence of an antiseptic element. On the banks of the Tarnbrook are a number of farms and a cottage selling honey with the bees feeding on the heathery slopes of the moorlands which the Duke of Westminster uses as a grouse shoot.

The source of the Tarnbrook is just above the hamlet of the same name which now consists of just a few cottages, farms and a Mountain Rescue Post which is often under pressure during the winter when thoughtless fell walkers take one risk too

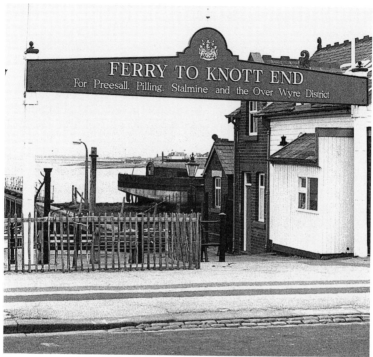

Entrance to the Knott End Ferry. Its future is now hopefully secure.

many. Tarnbrook is at the end of a cul-de-sac and was once described as a closed village specialising in the manufacture of hats using the pelts of rabbits, and especially moles. The pelts were cured by rubbing them with the salts of heavy metals, particularly lead and mercury. The skin of the worker softened by the grease from the pelts became absorbent to the salts and they passed into the bloodstream. We now know that these chemicals can cause brain damage, and the old saying 'As mad as a hatter' might well have some substance in fact.

Eventually both the Marshaw and the Tarnbrook lead down into Abbeystead which lies at the heart of what is now the estate of the Duke of Westminster with his agent's offices close to a bridge over the Tarnbrook. Although no evidence remains, there was once an attempt to establish a monastic settlement in this wild spot, by a group of brothers from Furness Abbey.

They abandoned the site and set up a sister house on the Isle of Man.

Here at Abbeystead are lovely old cottages fringed in spring by daffodils, a tiny school and a water fountain bearing the date 1892, all dominated by a magnificent horse chestnut tree which takes us back to a more leisurely age. The circular pinfold between the school and a farm is yet another reminder of rural life. Stray sheep were kept in the pinfold awaiting collection by their owners.

Here the Marshaw and the Tarnbrook join just before they enter a reservoir and it is the Wyre which emerges from the opposite end. At this point water crashes over a high dam and cascades down into a miniature grotto surrounded by trees beneath which grow a colourful tangle of spring and summer flowers. The Wyre was once a very important salmon river and a substantial ladder was built close to the dam to allow the fish access to their spawning grounds; this can still be an exciting spot to visit during a good run of fish. In winter the reservoir is a haven for a wide variety of wildfowl including a flock of Canada geese which is increasing each year.

Below the reservoir stands the so-called Shepherds' Church overlooking the meandering river and surrounded by rolling green fields. The official name for Over Wyresdale's parish church is Christ's Church but locals will always refer to it as the Shepherds'. There has been a church on this site since the fourteenth century when John of Gaunt gave £4 per year to support what was then described as a chapel. In 1733 it was rebuilt, although some arches and a couple of south-facing doors may be from the old chapel. The pulpit dates from 1684, and below this in a glass case is a fine example of a Geneva Bible printed around 1599. This one is known as a breeches bible because the word 'apron' in Genesis Chapter 3 verse 7 has been mistranslated as 'breeches'.

In the vestry is a collection of musical instruments, a reminder of the days when the church had no organ but did have its own small orchestra. There is plenty of interesting, mainly nineteenth-century, stained glass, all on the theme of the shepherd and his flock. In the outer porch is a rack on which shepherds can hang their crooks, and above this swallows nest every summer.

The Marshaw Wyre flowing past one of the farms and cottages which offer honey for sale.

As the Wyre flows into Dolphinholme the reason for the Abbeystead reservoir is at once evident – power for mills. At Lower Dolphinholme the Waggon Road leads down to the river near which is a derelict mill, and a row of restored cottages. It is spanned now by a solid bridge, but there are still signs of the old ford over the Wyre. The cottages seem to have very low

The salmon ladder near Abbeystead.

The Shepherd's Church at Over Wyresdale.

doors and windows, but this was not the fault of the original builders, merely an indication that when the bridge was built the old road down to the ford had to be raised. On the bridge and along the wall of the old mill are pipes and brackets, a reminder of the days of prosperity when the hard-working village was one of the first in Britain to have its own very rough-and-ready street lighting.

Downstream from Dolphinholme is Scorton picnic site and village. The 9-acre site, beautifully laid out, is under the control of the Lancashire County Council and is 3¼ miles north of Garstang. From Scorton village take the road towards Dolphinholme for about one mile before turning left at a brown sign. A bridge carries the road over the M6 motorway and the picnic site is on the left. There are frequent bus services from Preston to Lancaster. The stop to ask for is Hollins Lane which is around ¾ mile from the picnic site.

We once walked here in early May, but it felt more like a heatwave in mid-August. Young and old alike were seeking shade and cold drinks, the latter usually available from a nearby cafe. There is a mass of bluebells in spring and we should never take our bluebells for granted for they draw

The Old Toll House at Garstang with the toll gatepost still in position.

amazed gasps from foreign visitors. Bluebells have their centre of distribution here in Britain, and although the French, Dutch and Belgians know the plant, it is usually associated with coastal areas and never dominant as here in Britain. Familiarity in this case should not be allowed to breed contempt!

A circular path leads from the picnic site and follows the River Wyre for some distance before swinging to the right and returning to the car park. The river is on the left with a marshy area on the right. A wooden hide has been sited overlooking a shallow pond, and from this we watched a mute swan busy upending or waddling about in the shallows in search of food. We noticed how the bird skilfully avoided being exposed to bright sunlight and used the shelter of overhanging alder, willow and a mass of bullrushes. If blue is the colour of May, then this walk is dominated for most of the rest of the year by the yellow of gorse and broom. So long as you don't touch it, gorse is a delightful shrub and like the much less vicious shrub the broom is a member of the pea family. In the days before the advent of barbed wire gorse was planted in hedgerows to ensure that it was stock-proof. Folklore tells us that when gorse is out of bloom, then kissing has to stop! Fortunately for lovers

Tewitfield Locks on the Lancaster Canal with the M6 motorway running alongside.

there are three species of gorse in Britain and their flowering seasons overlap, which means that kissing can go on throughout the year, including winter!

If gorse has the folklore, then broom has the history! Its non-prickly branches were indeed used for 'brooms' and its scientific name is *Cytisus scoparius*, but it used to be called *Planta genista*. The coat of arms of Henry II (1155-1189) was emblazoned with a spray of broom pods, since his father hailed from an area in France where the plant is common. It is from the name of the plant that the Plantagenet kings took their name, and surely no other plant can boast such a history! It is said that a flower of broom slipped into wine by a lady would ensure that a man would be attracted to her. What with broom and gorse, the medieval world seems to have had little need for oysters, rhino horn or Chanel No. 5!

This is truly a naturalist's walk and we listed ground ivy, bugle, lesser spearwort, stitchwort, ramsons and red campion as well as the dominant bluebell. We remarked on how strange it was to be so near to the roar of the M6 motorway, and yet its sound was muted by the ripple of the Wyre over its bed of clean pebbles and the sound of birdsong. We heard blackbird,

Blackpool's Big Wheel being demolished in 1928.

willow warbler, chaffinch, blue and great tit, robin and wren, all of which we expected, but wood warbler and a persistent cuckoo were more surprising. In winter the hide can provide the watcher with regular sightings of mallard, teal, pochard, tufted duck and moorhen with the occasional great crested grebe, dabchick, snipe, and on one exciting occasion we watched a water rail pick its way among the icy margins of the

One of the Big Wheel carriages being loaded for removal to the Wyreside home of the Swallow sisters in 1928.

pond. In high summer we look upon this area as a paradise for botanists and butterfly watchers. In the margins of the paths jack-by-the-hedge is dominant and provides food for the larvae of orange-tip butterfly, whilst in the marshy areas and the pond grow water mint, water horsetail and the well-named arrowhead. The shape of the leaves of arrowhead varies according to the speed of the water in which they grow. In slow-moving water the leaves are broader, whilst in quick-flowing streams they are more narrow and pointed and provide the arrowhead with its common name. In the superstitious days of old, folk believed that because the leaves were shaped like an arrow they could be brewed up to produce a 'mush' used to treat wounds caused by arrows.

It is quite possible to spend the whole day around the river, especially for families with young children who can never resist dipping a net into a clean shallow river. From the narrow road near the picnic site a footpath leads off to Scorton village which is just over a mile away. The Wyre can be heard trickling its way on the right, whilst to the left of the track is a mass of brambles which are popular with those who enjoy a spot of 'living off the land'.

The Cartford Toll Bridge over the Wyre.

Scorton, although small, caters very well for visitors and the Priory Cafe was busy serving afternoon teas and the shop attached was doing a roaring trade in ice-cream and postcards. Opposite the Priory Restaurant on Snow Hill is St. Peter's Church which has a unique attraction for those who want to indulge in nostalgia. A small museum called 'Wendy's Memory Lane' has been formed in the basement of the vicarage. Descending the stairs, we were met by the sounds of the 1939-45 war with Vera Lynn very much to the fore. If you want to know what a grocer's shop looked like at that time, what clothes were worn, what it was like to wear a gas mask, how folk did their washing and so on, then this is the place. It is hard to believe that all this was set up by 'amateurs'. On the evidence of our visit they have much to teach some of the professionals, and Memory Lane should not be missed. The exhibition is open from 2pm to 5pm on Wednesday, Saturday and Sunday. A small fee is charged and helps with the church's running expenses.

Also rich in nostalgia is the ancient market town of Garstang. The main street is dominated by its market cross and town hall, the latter having to be reconstructed after a fire destroyed the 1750 building. This in its turn had been built to replace

The restored mill at Thornton.

another structure dating to 1680 which was also destroyed by fire. The town is of ancient origin, which is not surprising as it is close to a ford over the Wyre. In AD 597 a Saxon named

Fleetwood around 1895 photographed from the top of the grain elevator.

Garri had his base here, and by the time of the Domesday survey the name had gone through several variations to become Cherestank. Ekwall, an expert on English place names, suggests that this may derive from the Old Scandinavian words 'geirr' meaning a spear and 'stong' which means a pole, and thus we have a boundary mark. Garstang may therefore have been a boundary settlement.

A market charter was granted by Elizabeth I in 1597, and during the reign of Charles II in 1667 a Charter of Incorporation was granted and the Freed Borough could appoint eight councillors or burgesses one of whom was to be in control and given the name of Bailiff. This system eventually evolved into the Mayor and Corporation after the Corporation Act of 1886. In 1889 Garstang set up the Town Trust, and although since 1974 it has been part of the Borough of Wyre, the Trust still has a ceremonial function. The market cross is in the form of a Tuscan column surmounted by an orb of stone. First erected in 1754, the impressive cross with its surrounding steps was restored in 1897 to celebrate Queen Victoria's diamond jubilee.

The past and present activities of the town can best be appreciated by visiting the Arts Centre which was built in 1756 and was once the Town Grammar School. It is directly opposite the riverside car park which has good toilet facilities. Although long closed to full-time students, the centre is still a hive of

The North Euston Hotel is a fine example of the work of Decimus Burton.

industry and serves tea and biscuits to visitors and those who attend the astonishing variety of societies including natural and local history, light opera, brass band and the arts group who hold regular exhibitions. All this has been achieved without destroying the feeling that here was once a place of learning for the children of the townsfolk when Garstang was famous for its cattle and corn as well as for yarn, linen and cotton, all once part of a thriving cottage industry. There was also a busy fish market with the catch coming from the River Wyre itself and also from its food-rich estuary.

In its heyday Garstang was served by an important turnpike road, and on the outskirts of the town there is a restored toll house which still has its gate supports in place. The Lancaster Canal, which actually linked Kendal to Preston, passes through the town and it was only the local council's refusal to allow a railway link which prevented Garstang from developing further and why it is now such a delightful 'timewarp town'.

Just off Church Street is a canal basin where boats are now

Fisherman's Friend export to many parts of the world as shown in the variety of packaging.

tied up for the winter but which is summer seems to burst with energy and a riot of colour and variety of craft design. The basin is overlooked by Th'owd Tith Barn Restaurant, which has a stone at the rear dated 1710, the conversion having produced a fascinating place to eat at very reasonable cost. At one end of a long room is a huge fireplace which we love in winter when huge logs crackle and throw heat onto the flag floors and a delightful aromatic scent into the room. Furnished with long highly polished tables and bench seats taken from an old chapel, it always makes us feel as if we were dining in a medieval hall. The serving wenches reinforce this by wearing mob caps and frilly aprons.

But the Tithe Barn is more than a place to eat Lancashire hot pot and pickled cabbage, beef and Yorkshire pudding or ham and eggs – it should also be regarded as a museum in its own right. Suspended from the cruck beams is an amazing variety of kitchen and farm implements including ploughs, churns, urns, querns and butter-making equipment plus

The Fisherman's Friend tram ready for Blackpool illuminations.

displays of tools used by turners, coopers, wheelwrights and blacksmiths. Even the food is served from behind a bar supported on the wheeled chassis of a Victorian farm cart.

Up a flight of open stairs is a small room which houses a display of the history of the Lancaster Canal. The section between Tewitfield and Preston, a distance of 41 miles, was opened in 1797 and was designed to transport wood, coal, slate and lime. The main canal was constructed along one level and is now the longest lock-free stretch in Britain. No wonder it is popular with boaters who like cruising as opposed to operating lock-gate machinery! There is also the added bonus of seeing from close quarters the architectural skills of John Rennie, one of the greatest of all the canal engineers.

The town has no ancient church because originally Garstang was two settlements called Market-Town and Church-Town linked by a footpath but now severed by the modern A6, and considered as separate settlements. Both would originally have been dominated by the castle of the Greenhalgh family which controlled the vital river crossing. This stout pile was constructed on the authority of Henry VII, the first Tudor king who defeated and killed the Plantagenet Richard III at Bosworth Field in 1485. The Greenhalghs had backed the right side and were rewarded by a grant to build their castle. In the Civil War of the 1640s, however, they got it wrong and backed the Royalists, so when Parliament was victorious it was ordered that the castle should be demolished. Local farmers were not slow to make use of it as an unofficial quarry, and all that remains is the odd wall and an untidy heap of stones. Looking down from the grassy knoll on which the castle stood, one has a view of Castle Farm, an attractive building dating from the seventeenth century and constructed from the walls of the once-proud castle.

Between Garstang and Scorton is the attractive Gubberford Bridge with a rather unattractive tale to tell. The ghost of the White Lady takes us back to the time of the Civil War and the Cromwellian soldier Peter Broughton, who in 1644 was laying siege to the castle. Taking a breather from the siege, Peter was leaning over Gubberford Bridge when he was approached by a beautiful woman dressed in white. He recognised his wife who five years previously had left him for another man. She advanced towards her husband and put her arms about his neck when from out of the bushes sprang one Robert Rowton, a Cavalier captain to whom the girl was bigamously married. The Cavalier stabbed her in the breast, mortally wounding her. The pair, on opposite sides of the war, combined to bury the body by the bridge. Although Peter Broughton confessed to this deed on his deathbed, it is said that the ghost of the White Lady still haunts the bridge.

Often referred to as the 'Cathedral of the Fylde', St. Helen's, Churchtown is dedicated to the mother of the Emperor Constantine; she was much favoured by Celtic missionaries. Although there has been a church on the site since Saxon times, the present building is Norman in origin, but contains examples of masonry from almost every century since. The fact that the churchyard is almost circular suggests that it is Saxon, since this shape was typical of the period. The oldest parts of the church are the circular pillars to the north of the nave which date to around 1200, whilst the pillars of the south aisle are octagonal. This indicates that the church has been widened, and it certainly looks broad in relation to its length. At the west end of the south aisle is a fine thirteenth-century window, whilst the tower is probably early fifteenth century and has a perpendicular arch.

The original Tudor roof remains, as do substantial parts of two chantry chapels. The Lady chapel to the south of the nave, reached by two steps, was founded by Margaret Rigmalden who died in 1516. Even earlier is the Roger de Brockholes chapel founded in 1499. It may well be this chapel which has caused the church to be given cathedral status by the locals. The chancel is described as 'of the minster type' with skilfully restored flanking screens called a 'Parclose', and there are also some fine carved misericords beneath the seat. Under the east window of the aisle is a leper's 'squint' or window through which the afflicted could watch the services without infecting the healthy. There are also some interesting bits of furniture including a Jacobean wooden pulpit dated 1646 and a brass chandelier with a fascinating tale to tell.

Being so close to the River Wyre, the church was often subject to flooding and in 1746 the damage was so bad that it was actually decided to rebuild it. The builder, however, decided that it would be cheaper to divert the river and was rewarded for his efforts; from this windfall he donated the chandelier to the church. The old course of the river can be seen by following the footpath from the churchyard path which is lined by stately beeches down to the present river bed.

In Churchtown itself are the village cross and two old inns. Actually the cross is a rare example of an eighteenth-century dial post, which is a Tuscan column surmounted by a square block with a sundial on the southern face. What was the town clock of its day has been restored to full working order. The much-altered Punch Bowl Inn, renowned for its bar snacks, was once called the Covered Cup after the local Butler family whose coat of arms featured a communion chalice; they were prominent in the area for many years. The Horns Inn is still recognisable as a late eighteenth-century coaching inn which was an important stop on the road between Garstang and the Fylde coast before the bypass was constructed in 1935.

Between Churchtown and St. Michael's-on-Wyre, the river has never been 'trustworthy' and the local people have for centuries been terrified every time heavy rain raises the level of the Wyre. A recent management scheme has brought hope of safety at last from the 'blood water' which is thought by some to be the translation of the Celtic word Wyre. An even older flood bank was constructed from the bridge at St. Michael's and skirts the church. The Wyre is tidal up to this point. Hawthorn and bramble dominate the bank, and on the flood plain below mushrooms grow in profusion during the early autumn.

Michelscherche is mentioned in the Domesday Book and it is probable that the first church was founded here by Paulinus in AD 640. Inside the church hangs the long pendulum which swings away to operate the clock on the tower. There are many reminders within the church of the Butler family of Rawcliffe Hall, situated some six miles downstream of St. Michael's. Near the top of the tower are the initials H.B. standing for Henry Butler, and here also is the family shield depicting three wine glasses. In 1468 John Butler founded St. Katherine's Chapel which was restored in 1953, Coronation year. Whilst other repairs were being carried out in 1956 in the sanctuary, a fine fourteenth-century mural was uncovered. This suggests that at one time the whole of the interior walls would have been so decorated.

Those wishing to follow the history of the Butler family should visit Rawcliffe Hall which has been converted into a country club for those staying at the caravan site which is open from 1st March to 31st October. There is said to have been a house on this site since Saxon times but it is known that in 1154 the Butlers were in residence and were the Hereditary Cup Bearers to Henry II, which accounts for the coat-of-arms seen in the stained glass windows of the Hall as well as on the tower of St. Michael's Church. After centuries of dominance the Butlers of Rawcliffe lost influence and their home by their strict adherence to the Catholic faith. During the period prior to the Spanish Armada the Butlers gave sanctuary to Cardinal Allen. This 'troublesome priest' was born in 1532 at Rossall, now the public school on the ourskirts of Fleetwood and around seven miles from Rawcliffe. After being educated at Oriel College, Oxford he became a priest. If truth be told, Allen was more of a politician than a priest and he was active in trying to replace the equally bigoted but Protestant Elizabeth I.

Memorial to the Fleetwood fishermen lost at sea.

Whilst fermenting trouble, the Cardinal was obliged to hide at Layton Hall, Mains Hall, now a fine hotel, and also at Rawcliffe. It is small wonder that Elizabeth I wanted him dead because in 1558 he wrote that she was 'an incestuous bastard, an infamous, depraved, accursed, excommunicated heretic, the very shame of her sex, the chief spectacle of sin and abomination in this our age and the only poison, calamity, and destruction of our noble Church, a filthy, wicked and illiberal creature'. After such words it is amazing that Cardinal Allen managed to die in his bed after a short illness at the age of 63!

These lower reaches of the Wyre are surprisingly little visited by tourists, who tend to be seduced by the seaside resorts of the Fylde coast. It is a pity to miss two attractive toll bridges at Shard Bridge and Cartford and the chance to have a cup of tea and a snack at one of the most interesting cafes in the country.

The Big Wheel has been built on the end of Wild Boar Cottage. A carriage looking like a tramcar, once carried around on Blackpool's Big Wheel, or Ferris Wheel as it was known, has been joined to the cottage. Inside you can enjoy a home-made meal whilst looking at pictures of the Big Wheel before its demolition plus other reminders of the Pleasure Beach in the hey days between the two world wars. The carriage got here due to the kindness of the two Swallow sisters who ran the Blackpool orphanage. They bought Wild Boar Cottage which had been made for farm labourers from clay dug out from a pond. When the Big Wheel was demolished in 1928 the sisters bought one carriage, had it transported by horse and cart and tacked it onto their cottage. This gave them extra room to give the orphans a free holiday. The girls slept in the carriage and the boys in a tent on the lawn. Since 1985 the carriage has been a cafe and the owner told us that she is always pleased to see the Blackpool orphans who regularly return with their own children to bring back memories of the kindness of the Swallow sisters.

The two toll bridges make it possible to explore both banks of the Wyre. On the Knott End side naturalists are in their element with salt marshes and mud flats providing both roosts and feeding areas. Birds found include dunlin, redshank and knot, which may have been named after Canute, the king who failed to control the sea. The area probably takes its name from the birds roosting here. At Knott End itself is a wide beach, and a 2½-mile footpath leads eastwards to Pilling and another leads back upstream to Hambleton close to Shard Bridge. The Wyre has long been used as a shelter for ships and Wardleys Creek is still used by pleasure boats. Some historians have suggested that there was once a Roman port off Knott End and point out that a rocky outcrop seen at low water is what is left of the masonry. What is beyond dispute is that there was a Roman port in the area, and if it wasn't here, then where was it? In the second century AD Ptolomy produced a map which marked Portus Setantiorum. It is thought that the Romans were planning to invade Ireland, and this port would have been an ideal base from which to launch the invasion fleet. This may well have been the beginning of a connection between Ireland and the west coast: St. Partick landed near Heysham to begin his ministry (see Chapter 6). Near Knott End is an earthwork called Danes Pad which we feel is probably Roman, although Scandinavians did have some influence here, arriving from their base on the Isle of Man. The privately owned Hackensall Hall was built in Elizabethan times on land once under the control of a Norseman called Haakon. The nearby England Hill derives from Ekke Lund – meaning grove of oak trees on a hillside.

A chief reason for the Romans and the Scandinavians coming into the Wyre estuary, apart from the shelter provided, was the important salt deposits which also account for the modern ICI complex on the Fleetwood Bank at Thornton. Many complain about the presence of industry but conveniently forget that we all use its products and it provides work for many people. We love to stand above Shard Bridge at night and look across at Thornton with the lights of the ICI works reflected in the water of the river and looking like an old-time ocean liner.

Thornton does have one delightful link with the past. Marsh Mill was built in 1794, and as it is 110 feet (34 metres) high, it dominates the small town. Although it has not ground corn since the 1920s, it has been restored and is a tourist attraction during summer weekends. At Stanah near Thornton there is a large picnic area on the riverbank, and from here a footpath follows the river upstream to Skippool. This was once an important harbour from which there are good views of the Shard toll bridge. During the Civil War a party of 600 Royalists on the run forded the river here. All the little ports on the Wyre including Skippool are now backwaters used by pleasure yachts and are totally unsuited to bigger ships requiring deeper water. They are, however, lovely spots to picnic and boat-watch, with good-quality snacks available from riverside inns.

Fleetwood, one man's dream, was developed to provide the Wyre with a deepwater port, but even this has fallen on hard times in recent years. But is it as sad and depressed as some have suggested? Fleetwood to us means kippers, trams, fishing and, of course, Fisherman's Friends.

The Hesketh-Fleetwood family had lived at Rossall Point for centuries, their impressive home now forming part of Rossall School. In the 1830s Sir Peter Hesketh-Fleetwood had a dream as he watched the railway push its way towards the coast. He carefully studied the latest engineering techniques and formed the opinion that it was impossible to drive a line over Shap Fell into Scotland. He therefore employed the architect Decimus Burton – one of John Nash's best students – to design a town at the mouth of the Wyre. Burton had the right credentials as he had designed London's Regent Street as well as large areas of St. Leonards on Sea and Hove. At the terminus of the railway Burton designed the impressive North Euston Hotel and Hesketh-Fleetwood awaited the flood of passengers from London's Euston on their way to Whitehaven, the Isle of Man, Ireland and Scotland. Queen Victoria travelled to her holiday in Scotland via Fleetwood. The year 1847 looked like being a milestone in the new town's rapid development but it proved to be more of a millstone round its neck. Also in 1847 engineers actually succeeded in pushing the rail link over Shap and the quick route into Scotland ruined Sir Peter Hesketh. Fortunately the town developed the dual function of fishing port and seaside resort, but both of these enterprises have struggled in recent years. The Icelandic cod wars affected Fleetwood badly, and although some vessels still put to sea and the fish market still functions, both are shadows of their former glory.

The Fleetwood Museum, sited in the old Whitworth Institute in Dock Street overlooking the Wyre, shares premises with the town's library and provides a detailed history of fishing in the town. It was built by Benjamin Whitworth in 1863 as a meeting hall, reading room and a library. In 1887 Samuel Fielden bought the building which is now listed and gave it to the town as a library. There is a small entry fee and displays include photographs, exhibitions of deep-sea and inshore fishing plus a mock up of a trawler bridge with visitors able to handle the controls. It is open from Easter to the end of October from 2pm to 5pm except on Wednesdays.

Fleetwood's claim to world fame these days is due to the staggering success of a lozenge once used by the fishermen to ease sore throats and other bronchial complaints caused by the freezing cold mists of the Atlantic. 1865 was a good year for inventions: a six-mile oil pipeline was laid in Pennsylvania, Pierre Lallament invented the bicycle, and James Lofthouse, a Fleetwood chemist, invented a fluid by mixing liquorice, capsicum, eucalyptus and menthol. In rough seas, however, the bottles into which it was poured were soon broken. Lofthouse therefore soaked the liquid into a lozenge and soon his shop was unable to cope with demand. Still run by the same friendly family, the Fishermen's Friend now warms the throats of the world and even has excellent sales in Japan. The modern factory is very different from the old shop, but the basic product has not changed.

From our visits to Fleetwood we always return with a packet of 'Friends', several pairs of local 'kippers' and a feeling of optimism. Where else can you find a fresh sea breeze, have a long ride down the coast on a tram and buy fresh fish direct from a dock? In addition to all this Fleetwood still caters well for tourists and has a wide assortment of accommodation, entertainment and sports facilities. Our final view of Fleetwood, however, has to be from the memorial to the deep-sea fishermen erected on the front in 1987. It is in the form of a trawler gallows, which is the tackle once used to raise the full nets from the water. It commemorates the loss of 42 ships and more than 400 men this century. This is a proud, and despite its relatively recent origins, an historic town.

Knott End and Fleetwood are set on opposite arms of the Wyre estuary and the two are connected by a small ferry which in the late 1980s was forced to close. Fortunately it is now open again and its future secured. For a small fee the ten-minute crossing provides splendid views of old Knott End, young Fleetwood and the thousands of seabirds whose aerobatics delight even the most dedicated 'townies'.

CHAPTER 5

Lunesdale to Lancaster and the Sea

Kirkby Lonsdale stands on the banks of the River Lune and forms the boundary between Cumbria and Lancashire. On its journey to Lancaster, the river passes close to a number of unspoiled villages including Tunstall, Melling, Hornby, Brookhouse, Caton and Halton before reaching Lancaster. From this historic city the wide but shallow river becomes an estuary with Glasson Dock on one bank and Sunderland Point on the other. Visitors to Lunesdale will find few museums and amenities, but this is glorious countryside with well-marked footpaths leading from all villages and from Lancaster itself.

Whenever the Brontë family is mentioned we think of the Yorkshire village of Haworth with its sloping streets, fine church, and parsonage now serving as a museum. We think of the literary sisters strolling the moors towards Wycoller near Colne in search of inspiration. Too little attention is paid to the days when the girls attended the school for the daughters of clergymen at Cowan Bridge. This was founded in 1823 by the Reverend William Carus Wilson who was vicar of the church of St. John the Baptist at Tunstall, which was mentioned in the Domesday Book. It was well known to both Charlotte and Anne Brontë who walked to it across the fields each Sunday to worship, and ate their lunch in a gallery which at that time stood at the west end of the church. The school cottages at Cowan Bridge appear as Low Wood in *Jane Eyre,* whilst Tunstall church is referred to as Brocklebridge.

We approached the church, which in medieval times was dedicated not to St. John the Baptist but to St. Michael, along a path lined with flowers including giant bellflower, crosswort, germander speedwell, red campion, great stitchwort and bugle. Growing against the wall of the churchyard we found a clump of sneezewort which look like overgrown daisies, and which were once dried and the leaves brewed to produce a 'tea' which relieved colds and sneezes. 'Wort' is an old Anglo-Saxon word meaning a plant.

Tunstall Church – well known to the young Brontë sisters.

Over the porch of the church is a reminder of the part played by the men of Lunesdale in the Battle of Flodden against the Scots in 1513. Over the porch of the church is a sundial paid for by money from Brian Tunstall, one of the captains of the English army who is mentioned in Walter Scott's novel *Marmion*. The church has some connection with Thurland Castle, the home of the Tunstalls. At one time it was a fortified hall encircled by a moat, but it was dismantled by order of Cromwell following the Civil War during which Thurland held out for six weeks in support of the King. The final destruction of the old castle was caused by a fire in the early eighteenth century, at which time the present private residence was built to replace it. It is not open to the public.

Just beyond the castle is the junction of the roads connecting Kirkby Lonsdale, Ingleton and Melling. Here the River Greta, which rises on the slopes above Ingleton, joins those of the Lune at Greta Bridge, and there is a toll bridge which once controlled traffic along the turnpikes. Although the house has been demolished, there is another tucked away on a side road to Ingleton which still has its weathered toll board still in position. This junction of the Greta and the Lune was well known to the

Romans who had a camp nearby, and the stones from some of their buildings were incorporated into Tunstall church. In the windows of the north wall there is a stone commemorating the work of a Roman doctor and acknowledging the assistance of Aesculapius the god of medicine and the goddess Hygeia from whom we derive our word for cleanliness.

As we looked across the fields from the church towards Thurland, the whole scene was bathed in the gentle pink flush of sunset and bats wheeled in and out of the tower. There have been three churches on this site since Saxon times, but the present tower is mainly fifteenth century. We once watched a barn owl hunting near the church but apparently it is many years since this lovely white bird nested in the tower itself. As the sun finally set and the dew began to form on the leaves of the plants, we discussed the Roman doctor and wondered if he gathered the sneezewort to cure the soldiers in his care.

A friend of ours once described this area of Lunesdale as the 'valley of the churches', and the tiny village of Melling is also dominated by its ancient church. No one knows for certain when St. Wilfrids was consecrated, but although no record appears in Domesday, it is known that a church existed in 1066 and was either repaired or rebuilt in 1068. It stands on the western slope of an ancient earthwork called Castle Mount, and this explains why the chantry chapel dedicated to St. Catherine is eight feet higher than the nave, an almost unique architectural feature. There is plenty of evidence of early Norman stonework including an aumbrie and a hagioscope or leper's squint. Near the north door there are traces of an old wall painting, and close to this is a display of musical instruments used by the church orchestra, just as at the Shepherd's Church in Wyresdale, in the days before they could afford an organ.

Whilst the Lune itself is one of the most beautiful rivers in England, it also has some delightful tributaries, one of the prettiest being the Wenning which meets the main river near Hornby. During the days of coaching, Hornby was an important stop on the route between Lancaster and Kirkby Lonsdale. The Castle Hotel has altered very little since this time and the stables and the iron rings for tethering the horses are still there. On the side of the hotel halfway up the wall is a

This fine example of a toll house, although weathered, still has its toll board and gatepost in position. It is situated on the road between Greta Bridge and Ingleton.

bricked-up doorway. The coaches used to stop beneath the door and the passengers travelling on the top could enter the hotel through the high door. Many of our modern words and sayings derive from the days of the turnpikes. The rich could afford to travel inside the coach, whilst those of lesser income travelled on top and were known as outsiders. The seats in the middle of the top deck were safer than the outside seats because those who went to sleep on the outside were quite likely to drop off! At Hornby there is still a Post Horse Lane and the church, castle, cottages and hotel would still be recognised by travellers from the old turnpike days.

The church tower dominates the road and takes us back to 1513 and the bloody battle which took place on Northumberland's Flodden Field. There was a chapel rather than a church on the site from around 1300 which was controlled from Melling. Sir Edward Stanley, who lived at Hornby Castle, gained national recognition by his exploits at Flodden and Henry VIII created him Lord Monteagle. A new church was built in celebration with the tower bearing a relevant inscription. There have been many alterations since the sixteenth century but the mighty tower remains intact, and within the church are some interesting old crosses and gravestones.

The best view of Hornby Castle is from the bridge over the Wenning, where its dominant position can be easily appreciated. The site was occupied by the Romans and also later by a Viking warrior by the name of Horni from whom the present village takes its name. With the coming of the Normans, first the Montbegons and then the Harringtons established and consolidated the castle. The Harringtons fell on hard times during the Wars of the Roses which blighted much of the fifteenth century. Both father and son perished in the Battle of Wakefield of 1463. Then followed a period from which fairy tales are often made concerning the two heiresses left at the castle. The girls were cheated by their uncle James Harrington, but the dastardly deeds of the wicked relative came to the notice of King Edward IV who imprisoned Sir James and placed the girls under the care of Sir Thomas Stanley. He played an altogether more subtle game and married one heiress to his son and the other to his nephew,

At the Crook of Lune both the scenery and the salmon fishing are magnificent.

thus ensuring that Hornby was soon controlled by the Stanleys.

During the Civil War the castle, like many others, was knocked about more than a bit, and in 1713 the battered building was bought by the infamous Colonel Charteris who had been cashiered from the Duke of Marlborough's army. He did carry out some restoration work but little of this was in good taste and he was said to have dabbled in the occult. We feel he would have made an ideal subject for a Victorian melodrama. The building we see today is the work of Edmund Sharpe, who was educated at Sedburgh, and Paley who was one of the North West's most prolific architects of the nineteenth century. The restoration was planned around the ancient keep which would still be recognisable to the Monteagle family. The castle is not open to the public but is managed as an estate with apartments let within it and the surrounding woodlands used to rear pheasants.

On the opposite side of the bridge to the castle there is a most attractive footpath along the banks of the Wenning. We always make a point of walking this route in each season of the year. Looking through our diaries, we find that we have watched goosander in winter, common sandpiper in spring, mink (alas) and water vole (thank goodness) in summer and masses of migrating swallows and warblers in autumn.

95

Following the old turnpike road towards Lancaster, you see several well-preserved milestones, and one of the oldest toll houses in the country is still attached to a garage, the owners of which have restored it. It can now be hired for a holiday with a difference.

Just off the main road is the Crook of Lune car park. A footpath follows the old railway line which once led from Lancaster's Green Ayre station to Wennington and which was opened in 1849 by the North Western Railway Company. It was known as the Little North Western to distinguish it from the London North Western. It closed in 1966 during the Beeching cuts but the old iron bridge over the Lune still stands and the views along the river and across to Caton Mill are a delight. Before the coming of the railway this idyllic river bend, well named the Crook of Lune, was painted by Turner.

Caton Mill, a splendid old building now showing signs of its age, was built in 1783 and originally employed mainly children along with a few women. It had an apprentice scheme begun by the Hodgson family who, in 1814, sold the mill to Samuel Greg who was a relative. Greg had another mill, at Styal in Cheshire, which has been converted into a splendid museum, and we feel that a similar project would be ideal for Caton Mill. This was one of the first water-powered cotton mills and it was always vulnerable to flooding. On the side of the mill is a stone on which the flood levels over the years have been recorded. Another interesting feature to be seen in Caton itself are the fish stones beside Arkle Beck overlooked by an ancient oak tree. Despite its obvious age we think that the theory that this is a Druids' oak can be discounted. The stones were once used by the monks of Cockersand Abbey to lay out their fish caught in the Lune and its estuary which they sold to add to their coffers. The only refreshments served these days are from the old white-painted cottage restaurant on the opposite side of the road.

Caton has no church of its own but is served by St. Paul's Church at Brookhouse. Overlooking the old village, the church is mainly Tudor, but there was certainly an earlier establishment here and a twelfth-century Norman doorway has been incorporated into the west wall. It has been blocked up using old tombstones, some of which are thought to be those of

The flood marker on the side of the wall at Caton Mill.

crusading knights. Set into the bridge near the Black Bull, which serves excellent bar snacks, is a hollowed-out rock called the plaque stone. This is thought to be the spot where seventeenth-century villagers left their money soaking in vinegar to pay for the goods left there by the traders who wanted to avoid the pestilence.

For the energetic, by far the best way to reach Lancaster is to follow the footpath along the old railway line by the side of the Lune. A reminder of the past can be seen at Halton where the old station remains, its goods yard now used as a car park. It looks rather sad without its lines. A narrow bridge crosses the river whose deep pools are much favoured by salmon anglers, and leads to Halton's ancient church. This is overlooked by an ancient earthwork surmounted by a flagpole on which there was once a Norman castle, and in the churchyard is an eleventh-century carved cross. Within the church is a Roman altar. There is an unusual black and white half-timbered porch which is modern rather than ancient but there is no doubting the pedigree of the solid fifteenth-century tower. Opposite the church is the well-named Boat House built on the site of the old ferry across the river.

Any approach to the county town of Lancaster is usually dominated by the Ashton Memorial, and the money spent on its restoration has to be regarded as totally justified. Also visible from the M6 is the University which has now established itself as a seat of learning and culture. Its theatre and also the Duke's Playhouse in the city itself provide entertainment including ballet and the classics as good as any in the North of England.

The modern name 'Lancaster' derives from the Norman Lune-castre meaning the castle on the hill. The river is without doubt the reason for the prosperity enjoyed by the town for the best part of 2,000 years. St. George's Quay is seen at its best from across the river, whilst towering above and reached by a steep path are the Priory Church and the Castle. The finest building on the quay is the Customs House which since July 1985 has served as the Maritime Museum. The building was designed by Richard Gillow of the local furniture-making family, who had their own merchant vessels importing the mahogany for which they were famous. The Customs House was constructed of locally quarried stone and has been

Brookhouse village and St. Pauls Church.

described as 'the finest example of Palladian architecture in the North West.' Beautiful it may be, but it was also functional and its central long room was where merchants, captains and shipowners met to discuss cargoes and their distribution. An important, and at times annoying, room was the Collector's Office where the customs dues were paid. There were other smaller offices housing minor officials plus store rooms where seized merchandise was kept until all outstanding dues and bonds had been paid.

The building has been restored and only minor modifications have been carried out to house the extensive displays, whilst outside is the old fishermen's lifeboat *Sir William Priestley* which is one of a number of full-sized vessels on display. Fishing was an important local industry and its various facets are described in vivid detail with shrimping, cockling and musseling also illustrated. Outside on the quay, warmed by the surprisingly bright February sunshine, we talked to a shrimp fisherman from Morecambe who had brought his little vessel up river on the tide in order to service his engine, do a little painting and carry out other essential maintenance in the shelter provided by the harbour wall and the Customs House. He told us that not many shrimps are caught during the winter, the best months being September and October. It is always best to talk directly to the fishermen themselves but there is no doubt that the museum succeeds in recording the sound, sight and even smell of Lancaster's long association with the sea.

There are also displays concerned with the Lancaster Canal. It is possible to sit aboard a reconstruction of the *Waterwitch,* a horse-drawn packet boat which carried passengers in smooth comfort between Kendal and Preston at a speed of 10 m.p.h. This, in the days before the railways, was regarded as miraculous. The canal cuts through 57 miles of countryside but also passes through the heart of Lancaster. Built between 1797 and 1819, the Lancaster Canal is rightly regarded as one of John Rennie's masterpieces, the aqueduct carrying the canal over the River Lune being one of the wonders of the canal age. The packet service continued until 1846, and just as travellers along the turnpike roads were catered for by coaching inns, so hotels developed on the banks of the canals. There is a fine example on the Lancaster Canal at Bolton-le-Sands.

In the museum there is also a display describing the crossing of Morecambe Bay by coach. There is an area which displays the boat builder's craft – is it an art or a science? – with a comprehensive collection of the tools once used. Here also is a whammel boat, used for salmon fishing on the Lune. Surrounding panels tell the story of the fishing methods which are still practised today. Just down the quay from the museum is a small shop which sells salmon which is smoked on the premises. On the estuary itself another 'smokery' is situated below the harbourmaster's office at Glasson Dock. We never prepare a picnic when we are exploring the Lune, but buy a warm brown loaf, some farm butter from Lancaster market, and a bottle of Chablis. We are then ready for a few slices of Lune-smoked salmon.

In wet and windy weather a whole day can be spent in the Maritime Museum, which has a good exhibition of the wildlife of Morecambe Bay and another which describes the home life of the fisher families. There is a charming and cheerful reconstruction of a 1925 living kitchen all gleaming with polished black lead. How well we remember a similar set-up in the home of grandparents who were of a seafaring

The Plague stone set into a wall at Brookhouse.

background, and our lasting memories are of the smell and the flickering light of an oil lamp and the antimacassar mats which covered and protected the backs of the best rocking chairs and the sofa.

The museum has been extended into an adjoining warehouse which was constructed around 1780 and contains displays showing how tobacco, cotton and sugar were handled. Lancaster's ships ranged across the seven seas but were particularly concerned with the markets in Europe, the West Indies and America until the slave trade with Africa ceased. There is a cafe and a shop and the whole area is arranged in such a way that the disabled are able to enjoy the museum – not all such establishments are so thoughtful.

From St. George's Quay a narrow path ascends steeply between cottages and then along a leafy lane to the Priory Church of St Mary. The Priory and its near neighbour the Castle stand on the summit of the 110-feet (34 metres) hill overlooking a majestic sweep of the Lune, and the bridge carrying the traffic towards the M6 is clearly visible.

At one time there was a substantial Roman fort on this site, probably established by Agricola. No doubt there would have been a number of pagan temples here and it has been tentatively suggested that there may have been a Christian church here as early as 210 AD. When alterations were being made to the church in 1912 part of the apse – the east end of the building – was excavated and beneath it were found a number of small oil lamps. These bear the inscription XP which was a Christian marking. A more tangible reminder of the Roman occupation are the remains of a substantial bath house which was excavated in 1974. The church is open each day and there is a coffee shop and a surprisingly varied selection of books and literature on sale.

In the middle of the eleventh century Lancaster belonged to the Saxon Earl Tostig, the brother of King Harold who died on the battlefield at Hastings as William of Normandy conquered England in 1066. William gave vast lands including Lancaster to Roger of Poston (also called Roger de Poitou) who in 1094 'for the welfare of his soul gave to God and St. Martin the church of St. Mary at Lancaster'. This was given to a group of Benedictine monks from St. Martin of Seez in Normandy. The Priory grew wealthy but its buildings were devastated by the Scots in the early years of the fourteenth century although the resilient Benedictines regained their power and held it until they fell foul of Henry V. In 1414, the year before the historic battle of Agincourt, Henry grew impatient with English monasteries paying taxes to the French which were then used to arm his enemies. He therefore suppressed several Benedictine houses including Lancaster.

In the event this was a good thing for students of medieval priories, because Lancaster did not suffer, when Henry VIII dissolved the monasteries with much greater ferocity between 1536 and 1540. Instead of a ruin we can now explore an unspoiled priory church. Our favourite areas of the building are the carvings on the undersides of the medieval choir stall seats. They are called misericords. Some of them are very amusing and were perhaps the carpenter's way of poking fun at his mates or perhaps at a boss he didn't like by carving a grotesque. Unique possessions of the church are the Coptic crosses made of brass. They were brought back from Abyssinia in 1868, having been rescued from the Magdala arsenal whilst waiting to be melted down to make cannons! They are thought to date from the fourth or fifth century, are in perfect

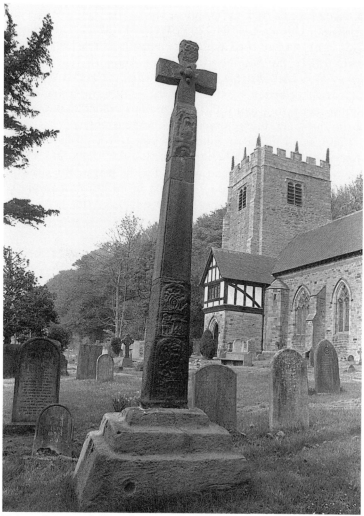

Halton Cross and Church – A quiet backwater very close to the busy M6 motorway.

condition and are inscribed with scenes from the gospels including the Nativity, Crucifixion and the Resurrection. The reason that the crosses found a place of honour in Lancaster is due to the King's Own Royal Regiment (Lancaster) 4th Foot having their memorial chapel here since 1903; their battle honours take us back to Namur in 1695. The regiment was also present at Gibraltar (1704-1705), Waterloo (1815), the relief of Ladysmith during the South African wars (1899-1902), Ypres (1915-1917), the Somme (1916-1918), Dunkirk (1940), Malta (1941-42) and Burma (the Chindits) (1944). What an impressive selection from a huge list – no wonder the chapel almost seems to groan with battle honours which make up one of the finest and most complete sets in the country.

There is so much to enjoy in a visit to the Priory that we always feel ready for a breath of fresh air to think and absorb the joys of this church, and we can feel its magnetism drawing us back. If this was the only building in the town, it would be worth travelling miles to see, but there is also a fine castle to be explored, not to mention the Museum in what was once the Judges' Lodgings.

Lancaster Castle is one of the finest in the country and we feel that there are two ways that it – or any other castle for that matter – can be explored. It is open to the public on weekdays when the courts are not sitting and also on summer weekends. One can treat the building in chronological order or enter through the main gate and follow a marked path. The second is the better at Lancaster since entry to some parts is restricted as it still functions as a gaol. The gatehouse was constructed during the early years of the fifteenth century as a precaution against the repeated attacks of the Scots. Although it is called John of Gaunt's Gateway, it was actually built by his son who, in 1399, became Henry IV as well as the Duke of Lancaster. The Duchy of Lancaster has been linked with the Crown ever since, hence the toast 'The Queen, the Duke of Lancaster'. The second tower to the right of the gatehouse is the Well Tower and this was where the Pendle Witches were imprisoned during their trial and prior to their execution in 1612. The majestic banqueting hall, The Shire Hall, and the courtrooms are imposing, but the Castle also had its areas of squalor. The turfed area in front of the Castle was once a jumble of cottages and one of a pair dating to 1739 has been preserved and furnished as an artisan's house of around 1820. Other old cottages have been converted into flats, others into offices, and one carries a plaque recording that it served as the town's dispensary between 1785 and 1832; the original apothecary's

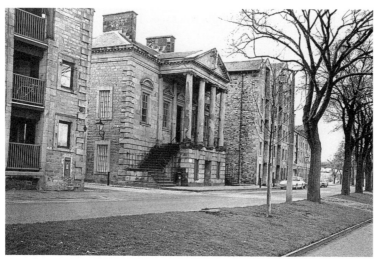

Lancaster's Museum, now one of the most informative maritime museums in Britain. The impressive building was once the customs house.

stone plaque depicting the good Samaritan has been transferred to the front door of the Royal Infirmary.

The Judges' Lodgings Museum situated at the head of Church Street is one of the most varied and informative in the county. It was built as a private house by Thomas Cavell in the 1620s, but it was purchased in 1820 by the Lancashire Justices to provide rich accommodation for the circuit judges sitting at the assize court in the Castle when the trials could often be of very long duration. His Lordship's bedroom has been recreated with an ornate bed and mahogany furniture, much of it, as you would expect, fashioned by Gillow. In an ongoing process the second floor is being set up as a typical period 'town house'. The Gillow Collection is fast becoming one of the best exhibitions of its type in the country. Another important area is the splendid Museum of Childhood. This includes the Barry Elder Doll Collection which was once kept at Carr House near Tarleton (see Chapter 2). There is also a schoolroom with bench seats, blackboards and slates which bring memories flooding back to those well past their youth, whilst the children love the ever-changing display of toys, games and books. There is a coffee shop and a delightful garden in which visitors can sit on hot days.

From the Castle, steep streets descend to the old Market Square, where in 1651 Charles II was proclaimed King, although it was not for a further nine years that he was able to rid himself of the Commonwealth of Cromwell. If political history was made in Lancaster, then it also played its part in industrial history, and to discover the details of this a journey should be made to the east of the town which is dominated by the Ashton Memorial. This is often all that travellers along the M6 motorway see of Lancaster – of the town itself they do not even know enough to realise what a joy they are missing.

The Ashton Memorial was saved from the brink of extinction in the late 1980s. It stands looking out over the 38 colourful acres of Williamson's Park given to the citizens by the father of James Williamson. James was born in Church Street in 1842, by which time his father had built up a sound business, manufacturing oil cloth. James proved to be even more astute and when he died in 1930 he had amassed a fortune of £9.5 million, had also given a great deal of money to his native town and had been its major employer for many years. He was a forceful M.P. and deserved his elevation to the peerage, taking the name of Lord Ashton. He gave Lancaster a Town Hall, a statue of Queen Victoria in Dalton Square and the memorial in the park which his father had given but which was substantially developed between 1877 and 1882. The Ashton Memorial was originally designed by John Belcher, and by 1904 his first plan was ready for consideration. Between 1907 and 1909 Belcher's partner had modified the design and convinced the client that here was a fitting memorial to his family. It rises over 220 feet (67 metres) and the view over the Lune valley from its dome can be literally breathtaking. The river sweeps down to the sea between the contrasting ports of Glasson Dock and Sunderland Point.

In retrospect it is difficult to imagine that the destruction of the memorial could actually have been seriously contemplated. It was certainly in a very poor state in 1984, but a steering group was set up and chaired by the Lord Lieutenant of Lancashire. The very best advice was taken, money was raised and sensibly spent, and the results are now apparent for all to

The Priory Church at Lancaster.

see. Displays and audio-visual presentations depict Lord Ashton's life as well as the age in which he lived. A 20-minute-long audio-visual display tells the life story of Edward VII.

In the park itself are a cafe, bookshop and the magnificent old Palm House which has been converted into a warm and comfortable butterfly enclosure. What a joy it is to leave the breezy top storey of the Memorial and enter the humid tropical heat of the old Palm House with its butterflies from South and North America, Australia, Africa and Asia. British species are not neglected either and there are programmes for breeding rare species.

Many common butterflies can be seen from the Nature Trail which runs from St. George's Quay to Glasson Dock following the route of the now closed railway line. The best way to explore this, however, is to travel by road to Glasson Dock or Conder Green where there are ample parking places, toilets and picnic sites.

Glasson is a sheltered harbour on the estuary of the River Lune which is still used for commercial purposes, including the transport of coal, but the marina is a haven for seagoing pleasure craft heading through the locks and out into the Irish Sea.

There are also a number of smaller craft which journey in

the opposite direction up the canal, which is a branching arm of the Lancaster to Kendal system. There are ample parking, toilet and refreshment facilities. The marina itself is a popular sanctuary for wildfowl, especially during spells of heavy weather, and the muddy coastline usually carries an interesting selection of waders, although the counts are seldom dramatic.

The surrounding salt marshes are equally popular with birdwatchers and botanists who seek out such plants as sea purslane, scurvy grass, sea aster, thrift, bittercress, orache and whitlow grass, while spurrey, sea lavender and sea sandwort provide autumn colour as well as edible seeds for the birds. Most bird species, however, use the salt marsh as a roost before emerging to feed on the mud flats.

From Glasson Dock a footpath follows the route of the old railway line which connected the dock to Lancaster via Conder Green, which also has ample parking and toilet facilities, including provision for the disabled. Cyclists and horse riders also use the track, which is lined with a wide variety of native trees on which feed several species of butterfly and moth. In the summer their caterpillars are fed upon by whinchat, stonechat, dunnock and several other passerine species. The path continues to St George's Quay at Lancaster, a distance of 4½ miles. Along the length of the walk are a number of picnic tables and sheltered spots overlooking the area.

Before a final decision was made, a number of schemes were discussed to run a line to Glasson Dock. In September 1845 the Preston and Wyre Railway Company put forward plans to connect Lancaster with Fleetwood with a branch running to Glasson. They did not have things their own way, however, and only a month later the York and Lancaster Railway proposed a line from Lancaster to Thornbush, which was close to Glasson, and there they wished to construct a new complex of docks. Neither of these schemes ever got off the drawing board and a railway did not actually begin operations until 1883. The line was constructed in three sections. These were Glasson Dock to Marsh (about four miles), Marsh to St George's Quay (about ½ mile), and then on to Lancaster Castle Station (about 1 mile). The only public station was at Glasson Dock, although one was constructed later at Conder Green and there was a private stop

The choir stall seats within the Priory Church have some of the finest and most amusing carvings to be seen anywhere in the county.

for Lord Ashton near his Hall – now Lancaster Golf Club's headquarters.

After nationalisation in 1948 the authorities mentioned closure, but it was 1969 before the line ceased to function altogether after years of declining trade. Most of the track which was single line has been taken over by nature and is a fine footpath, surprisingly well drained and a good walk in all seasons. 'I love these railway walks', a friend once confided to us. 'You know you aren't trespassing and there's no way you can get lost'.

When visiting Glasson, time should be taken to view Thurnham Hall and Cockersand Abbey, although care should be taken not to trespass on private land. A sweeping drive through green pastures leads to Thurnham Hall, built around a fourteenth-century pele tower and backed by wooded gardens and an avenue of yews. The Dalton family (a hotel at Glasson Dock is named after them) lived in the hall for more than 400 years and were responsible for some attractive Elizabethan extensions, a fine Jacobean staircase and some good panelling and plaster work. The Gothic-style chapel and a cunningly placed priest's hole reveal a connection with the Catholic church and especially with the nearby Cockersand Abbey. Although the hall has been divided into a number of flats, the character of the Daltons' hall has been largely retained.

A lane opposite Thurnham Hall descends from the main road down to the old lighthouse, and beyond this is what remains of Cockersand Abbey. In our explorations we have been lucky in that our friends Mr and Mrs Gerrard live at Crook Farm close to the Abbey and much of its stonework is incorporated into their milking parlour. The house also has a number of monastic arches and windows. The abbey was built by the Premonstratensians in 1190 and initially the buildings covered an area of more than an acre but most has been gradually eroded by the sea. You can still see signs of the cloisters, and the chapter house dating from 1230 is remarkably well preserved as it was used by the Dalton family as a burial chapel. Close to the disused lighthouse is what at first sight seems to be a pile of masonry, sometimes lapped by the sea. This is all that is left of the monastic fish trap designed to catch salmon.

Looking at what remains of the Abbey today, it is difficult to imagine that, of the twenty or so monasteries which existed in Lancashire, Cockersand ranked third in wealth and influence. It began as an isolated hermitage, but by the reign of Henry II (1154-1189) it had been 'upgraded' to a hospital for aged monks from an abbey in Leicester. William de Lancaster, Baron of Kendal, and the Fleming family gave much land to the Abbey which included Pilling Moss, and then as now it was rich in wildfowl which provided a good income. In those days a bird catcher was employed by all landowners and he filled the role of the modern butcher. In 1190 Pope Clement ordained the house and named it St. Mary of the Premonstratensian Order of Cockersand.

It was dissolved in 1537 but was granted the very rare privilege of re-foundation, but this was short-lived and two years later the seal was finally broken. The plate was taken for the King and the furniture was sold, the pieces having in the intervening centuries been distributed throughout the county and beyond. Although almost all the Abbey has gone, there are

The Gatehouse at Lancaster Castle.

few more impressive buildings that the chapter house from which there are splendid views of Overton and Sunderland Point.

These can only be reached by returning through Lancaster and following the road first to Morecambe and then turning left towards Middleton. The road is often covered by the tide and so motorists have to be careful. There is, however, an interesting inn which offers shelter to the stranded. Officially called the Golden Ball, this is known by the locals as 'Snatchems' and is said to relate to the days when the press gangs raided the area, and to get a crew they simply 'snatched 'em'. We once spent a happy week here making a film about the River Lune, and during that time we watched fishermen 'whamelling' and learned to use a Haaf net. This is a Scandinavian method of fishing with a framed net looking like a set of football goalposts. These are carried over the shoulder and the fisherman then walks into the sea, which for us required a deal of courage and confidence in the teacher. The net hanging down catches the salmon by trapping the gills and is secured by a twisting movement. Many of the salmon smoked at Glasson Dock and Lancaster have been caught by this method.

Glasson Dock on a typically busy day with the Dalton Arms, named after the local Lords of the Manor, in the background. Here are fine Lancashire ales and substantial bar snacks.

Beyond 'Snatchems' is the village of Overton which has an interesting inn and an ancient church. The Ship Inn looks like an old English pub with low beams and small rooms and it serves substantial bar snacks. In Victorian times, when such activities were legal, the landlord of the inn amassed a huge collection of birds' eggs and stuffed specimens. These are still a feature öf the inn and the wall-mounted wooden cases are of typical Victorian workmanship.

The parish church of St. Helen is one of the most ancient in Lancashire. The Anglo-Norman doorway has been ascribed to the period between 1050 and 1140. The west wall, built of gritstone and around 4 feet (1.3 metres) thick, may well be Saxon. Our favourite view of the interior is from the gallery which was built in the early eighteenth century and may have been constructed for the orchestra. The view from the churchyard across the Bay is delightful with Cockersand and Glasson Dock being prominent.

From Overton a causeway runs across to the old port of Sunderland and is covered by every tide, giving the settlement a feeling of splendid isolation. In the eighteenth century the

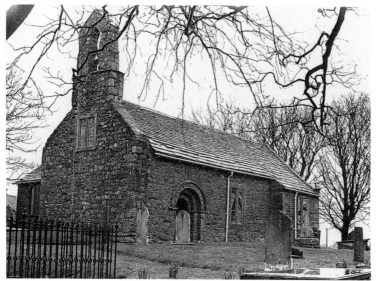

Overton Parish Church.

Quaker, Thomas Lawson, developed the port to trade with the West Indies, and it is said that the first cotton to be imported into Britain came here. The old warehouse has been tastefully converted into cottages but the so-called 'cotton tree' still seems to be growing out of the wall. This is actually a Kapok tree the seeds of which probably arrived snuggled in a bale of cotton. Thomas Lawson overstretched himself and became bankrupt, the port fell into disuse and apart from weathering has changed little since.

It is always worth standing at the Point in winter and watching the sea between Sunderland and Glasson. Cormorants are regular but red-throated and great northern divers are also spotted with reasonable regularity. To the non-ornithologist Sunderland Point has a unique attraction in the form of the grave of Sambo, a negro slave reputed to have pined to death at the disappearance of his master. He is buried behind a wall in unconsecrated ground and local children provide him with a regular supply of wild flowers. On winter days of high wind and heavy rain Sambo's wall provides shelter for those watching the birds on the marsh. His is a more

Sunderland Point in the 1940s – and has changed little since. The warehouse on the left has been converted into flats, but the so-called 'cotton tree' still stands and looks much the same.

peaceful resting place than most folk buried in churchyards could ever have hoped for.

The view from the grave reveals Middleton Holiday Camp, part of the Pontins complex, beyond this is the Heysham power station and village, and beyond these is Morecambe.

CHAPTER 6

Around Morecambe and Heysham

Morecambe developed from a small fishing village into an important seaside resort during the Victorian period when steam trains brought visitors from the textile towns of Lancashire but especially from Yorkshire. It quickly outgrew the more ancient and historic Heysham, but this developed an important harbour linking to Ireland and the Isle of Man. After a period of decline Morecambe is beginning to get to grips with tourism of the 1990s but many now point an accusing finger at the nuclear power station at Heysham.

Nuclear Electric are at pains to defend themselves against ill-informed criticism although they do realise that safety must be high on their agenda – indeed nothing should take precedence over this. There are two reactors at Heysham which are the most advanced in the country and will continue to operate well into the twenty-first century. Both are powered by Advanced Gas-Cooled reactors (AGRs) and Heysham generates sufficient power to supply the whole of Lancashire and most of Greater Manchester. The visitors' centre is open all the year round except Christmas Eve and Boxing Day. Tours of the power station are organised each day and children are welcome. In the centre is a cinema and a continually evolving display showing how the power is generated. We feel that tourists should not fail to visit the power station as it is part of local life and they may well feel that the industry is not so black as it is often painted. They will, in fact, find that Nuclear Electric are surprisingly green. We visited the observation tower which overlooks the harbour, the power station itself and Morecambe Bay. Far out at sea on a good day it is possible to see the gas rigs, yet another method of generating energy which is frowned upon by conservationists. We feel obliged to point out that it is impossible for us to manage without power and it is also impossible to generate power without some risk, however theoretical. The work provided for local people is also an important factor which should not be ignored.

A nature trail has been laid out through the grounds of the power station which is freely open to the public. The local ornithologists have been provided with a work centre and the ringing station is of increasing importance. From here sea and estuary watches are organised and three hides overlooking the station's outfalls have been sensibly located. Two have been constructed from ship cargo containers with windows cut into them and seats bolted inside them. They have been secured so firmly into the harbour wall that even the storms of January and February 1990 failed to disturb them. We have spent many happy hours in these hides including one day in June when we watched a female red-breasted merganser sail majestically past with fifteen chicks in tow behind her. The local experts know well that sea hides are best visited at times of high wind when the wildfowl, water and seabird counts can be exciting, especially at the point where the hot water outfalls are situated. Most naturalists are realists and they know that bird counts have been made here long before the power station was built. These are being continued and in time the comparative figures may be used to detect any impact on the environment, and an annual report is produced. The reserve also provides for the young and the Field Studies Centre is frequently used by schools. Pond dipping is the main activity, but botany and the study of butterflies, moths, birds and small mammals are all an important part of the facilities provided.

Those in search of Lancashire's history should not allow the presence of the power station or the harbour to detract from the beauty of Heysham, one of the finest examples of an ancient village in the whole of Britain. This has changed very little over the centuries and St. Patrick would probably recognise part of the view of Morecambe Bay from the ruins of the little chapel dedicated to him.

The weather was threatening as we made our way towards St. Peter's Church, and although it was February, the churchyard was a mass of predominantly purple crocuses. We went first up onto the headland where the yellow blooms of gorse nodded in the stiff cool breeze. Across the Bay we could see the cranes of the Barrow shipyards and also the stark scaffold-like structures of the oil rigs. A flock of redwings headed out into the Bay, the sands of which had been exposed

Heysham A and B, two modern nuclear power stations.

as the tide ebbed. Redshank, curlew and shelduck fed eagerly in the shallow pools left behind.

St. Patrick's Chapel is perched on a rocky outcrop and was founded by Irish Christians during either the sixth or seventh centuries, and it seems highly likely that this is Lancashire's oldest religious house. It is only around 24 feet long by 7 feet wide (7 metres × 2.2 metres), and in what was once the churchyard 'body-shaped' graves have been hacked out of the rock – the soil was probably so shallow that digging a grave would not have been possible.

The present parish church dedicated to St. Peter and situated below the chapel is also set on an outcrop. There can be few buildings so beautifully sited with views over the Bay towards Morecambe, and the church also has an interesting and historic interior. An efficient central heating system welcomed us as we examined the curved hogsback tombstone which has Christian symbols on one side and Scandinavian pagan symbols on the other. This is possibly an example of a converted Viking making sure that he did not offend either his old or his new God. The south-west doorway and west window are probably Saxon, and there is also plenty of evidence of the adding of a Norman church onto a Saxon framework round about 1080. There is an early Norman arch in the chancel which has rope-like mouldings, which were probably there because St. Peter was a fisherman. There have been additions

117

The observation tower provided by Nuclear Electric, from which there are splendid views over Heysham Power Station and the birds' muddy feeding grounds along the coast.

to the church in most centuries since, including the bellcote added in the seventeenth century and the north aisle which was surprisingly sensitively constructed in 1864.

In the summer the narrow street is thronged with visitors, the large car park fills up, genteel tea shops do a roaring trade and gallons of the local delicacy, nettle beer, are drunk. Tasting a little like ginger beer, the recipe for nettle beer is said to be a carefully guarded secret. As we have seen, even the presence of the nuclear power station can now be regarded as an extra tourist attraction, like Sunderland Point described in Chapter 5.

In his book *Lancashire Plain and Seaboard,* published in 1953, Herbert C. Collins wrote, 'None of the major sea-bathing towns of Lancashire can offer such glorious scenery as Morecambe. The bay is shapely and spacious with, as a background, the Lakeland and Pennine mountains which are close enough to play their part in providing a constantly changing pattern of light and shade according to the weather.' How right he was, and in the following forty years little has changed, and although we spend a lot of our time in the resort, it can still provide us with unexpected patterns of light over the sea. From the shore can be seen Black Combe (1969 feet – 600 metres) which is too small to be a true mountain, but sweeping right from its smooth slopes are views of Haycock and Harter Fell, Seathwaite Fell, Walna Scar, Scafell, Dow Crags, Coniston Old Man and Great Gable.

Humphrey Head stands out into the sea near Kents Bank, and behind this rise Wetherlam and the Langdale Pikes. Behind Grange-over-Sands lies Helvellyn, and to the right is Fairfield, and as the eye sweeps eastwards and southwards, the Howgills and the Pennines come into view. These views are at their best during the autumn when the pink of the setting sun outlines the crests of the mountains; in rough weather it is difficult to take the eyes off the sea and the coastguards need to be diligent as far too many surfboarding enthusiasts ignore warnings and risk their lives even when the red warning flag is flying.

This unique landscape, however, played no part in the early development of Morecambe which evolved for two reasons. Firstly there was the developing nineteenth-century craze for sea bathing and secondly the desire by early railway companies to set up reliable connections and sailings to Ireland; Morecambe was able to provide both. Prior to this there was no such place as Morecambe but there were four villages straddled along the coast – Poulton-le-Sands, Bare, Torrisholme and Heysham. A suitable year from which to date the beginning of

Morecambe is 1820. Poulton-le-Sands was then a small fishing village with a population of around 360 administered from Lancaster about three miles away. In this same year a building called Morecambe Cottage at Poulton was advertised as 'To let as a base for sea bathing', thus anticipating the future name of the resort.

We always enjoy watching the birds at Morecambe including turnstone, sanderling, dunlin, oystercatcher, redshank and curlew feeding among an amalgam of mud, shingle and sand. There are a few visitors here even during the winter, and they are often able to sit and drink their flasks of coffee on the promenade seats overlooking the mudflats. During one bird watch in early March the crocus and daffodils were blooming, and although the gardens were not so colourful as in high summer, they were still pretty. The end of the pier was still being lapped by water and the shrimp boats were bobbing in tune to the rhythm of the waves. Morecambe seems able to accommodate fishermen, historians and visitors with ease, and however often we write about it, there is always some new sight, sound or colour to be described.

Looking at the resort today, it is difficult to see it as a port, but around 1850, Poulton-le-Sands handled twice the cargo of Glasson Dock and did not have the worrying problem of silting, which was always a problem with the ports of the Lune estuary including Sunderland Point, Lancaster and Glasson. At Poulton a railway station was constructed on the stone jetty and provided a base for a direct trade link with Scotland but more especially Ireland. This project was short-lived, however, because during the 1860s the Furness railway developed a better port, first at Roa Island near Barrow-in-Furness, now in Cumbria, and then the developing shipbuilding town itself. The final death knell came to the Port of Morecambe with the successful development of Heysham. Was the Morecambe enterprise a total failure? Indeed it was not, since the rail link had already begun to ferry visitors to enjoy the sea bathing. Many trippers came from the industrial towns, especially the Yorkshire woollen towns, and Morecambe soon became known as Bradford-by-the-sea. Visitors had already begun to call the expanding resort after the lovely bay in which it nestled. In 1881 a publication called *The Topography and Directory of*

Morecambe Promenade in 1895.

Lancaster and 16 miles around reported 'Poulton-le-Sands, now better known as Morecambe, is a clean, healthy and popular watering place ... with numerous well appointed shops, inns and lodging houses for the reception and accommodation of visitors and tourists, for whose use there is a large supply of vehicles and pleasure boats.'

Morecambe, however, still had the dilemma of whether it should be looking towards the beauties of the Lake District or copying the brash exhibitionism of Blackpool which was far too close and much too ambitious for comfort.

Morecambe meantime retained its link with its shipping origins in the shape of Ward's shipbreaking yard in the centre of the promenade.

Shipbreaking may be dirty and unglamorous but it confirms the old adage 'where there's muck there's brass'! Not only were brass, copper, steel and many other metals sold off for recyling in furnaces around the country, but holidaymakers to Morecambe paid 6d a time to look around the ships. In the 1920s the yard attracted nearly half-a-million visitors, making it a major tourist attraction and earning Wards many thousands of pounds.

The yard employed up to 200 men after the First World War

when the navy disposed of its surplus ships. In total, approximately 60 vessels were broken up at the yard. They included dredgers, destroyers, oil tankers, cargo ships and German submarines.

Famous and unusual vessels included the huge German battleship *Heligoland* (22,440 tons) in 1922 and the cruiser HMS *Glasgow*, which took part in the Battle of the Falklands (1914) and was one of the fastest ships in the navy. The star of the show was the Blue Riband White Star liner *Majestic*, which arrived for breaking in 1914.

Morecambe was the third shipbreaking yard opened by Wards. The first of these 'depots', as they were called, were established at Preston and Barrow in 1894. The success of the Sheffield-based firm made it the largest scrap business in the U.K., responsible for many large and prestigious projects including dismantling the burned-out Crystal Palace and the ill-fated airship R101 in the 1930s. The Morecambe yard closed in 1933 after the railway-owned site was sold to Morecambe Corporation.

We can remember visiting Morecambe in the days when tourists came via Lancaster Green Ayre Station, the line to Morecambe being electrified as early as 1908. This was operated by the Midland Company who built Promenade Station in a stately style and also constructed the impressive Midland Hotel, which was given an thorough facelift in 1990. All this was greatly appreciated by the Yorkshire folk who travelled the delightfully scenic route via Settle and then down the Lune valley to Lancaster. Other railway companies also ferried in visitors and the London and North Western had its terminus at the much more austere Euston Road station.

What did Morecambe have to offer sun and sensation seekers in competition with Blackpool? Blackpool had – and still has – its tower, but in its time Morecambe had two, neither of which stood the test of time. The first tower was a revolving and rather too delicate structure which folk saw as they came out of the Promenade Station, but the second was much more solid and ambitious, and in retrospect it is difficult to see why it did not succeed. It was situated close to the Central Pier (Morecambe had only two despite the name of central) on the site now occupied by Granada Bowl. The Morecambe Tower

St. Peters Church, Heysham.

Company was set up in 1898 with a capital of £70,000, and with spectacularly ambitious plans laid out in a glossy prospectus: 'A tower of 232 feet high upon a scale somewhat different in construction to the towers of Blackpool and Paris. The tower will have a diameter of about 150 feet at the base gradually diminishing to a platform of 52 feet in diameter at the summit, upon which will be a large refreshment room. A spiral road round the outside will gradually ascend by easy gradients from the ground to the platform, which may also be reached by an electronic tramway or hydraulic lifts.' These imaginative plans never came to total fruition: the tower had to be ascended by ladders and was also later damaged by lightning. During the First World War the metal on the upper framework was dismantled and used to make armaments. The lower pavilion section was designed to seat up to 5,000 people in comfort and was not finally demolished until 1959 when it was replaced by an Amusement and Bingo Hall.

Both Blackpool and Morecambe had their own Winter Gardens with Morecambe doing its best to outdo Blackpool, the massive terracotta building having lush interior seating and glittering chandeliers. The two resorts also competed for the most splendid theatres and hotels. Morecambe had the magnificently ornate Royalty Theatre designed by Frank Matcham who also designed many other theatres including the Grand in Blackpool. Although Morecambe theatres in their hayday compared favourably with those at Blackpool, the same cannot be said of the hotels, although there were two notable exceptions – the Midland and the Broadway. The latter has been described as Mrs Bourne's Masterpiece and had five storeys, whereas in 1936 the normal arrangement was to have only three. It was set into a corner site with a colonnaded entrance porch. Many of the 1930s features have been retained including the sunburst leaded lights in the upper parts of the window frames.

Like many of Britain's seaside resorts, Morecambe went through a period of depression as its traditional customers went on package holidays to Spain in search of a reliable period of hot sun. Because the workers constructing Heysham Power Station required lodgings the traditional boarding houses providing good cheap accommodation managed to survive whilst similar establishments in other resorts were forced to close. This gave Morecambe the breathing space to plan leisure facilities independent of the weather such as the Bubbles Leisure Park with a tropical indoor fun pool. There is also a wave machine which delights the children. Frontierland is a theme-park area with country and western shows, an indoor complex, bars and restaurants plus more than thirty traditional fairground rides. Throughout the 1990s Morecambe is planning to widen its appeal by organising festivals of music and jazz, carnivals and summer shows. The resort has never been afraid to copy ideas from other resorts but has also been an innovator itself. It was the first resort to organise illuminations, and the Promenade and Happy Mount Park are a blaze of colour from mid-August to the end of October. This successfully extends the season, and many people now have one holiday in the sun and another autumn break when they hope for and often get an Indian summer. When Marineland Oceanarium opened, it was the first of its type in Europe.

The early 1990s have brought problems for the Pier with entrepreneurs competing with each other in the production of

Ward's shipbreaking yard at Morecambe in 1921. The vessels from left to right are HMS *Mersey, Adventure,* the *Kempelfelt, Pexton Diadem* (a cruiser), and almost broken up the cruiser *Hans Albion* and the German submarine U 101. (By courtesy of the Lancaster City Museum).

refurbishment schemes to take the resort into the next century. One thing is certain – Morecambe, as a lively resort cannot afford not to retain its Pier.

Morecambe has now realised its role for the next century. As tourism becomes more organised, it has the accommodation to satisfy the increasing number of visitors who wish to explore the nearby Lake District as well as the chain of small villages around Britain's largest estuary – Morecambe Bay.

CHAPTER 7

Morecambe Bay

We have often heard Morecambe Bay described as an area of wasteland covered for half the time by the tide, but we always ask the question 'Waste to whom?' It is certainly not a waste area to the many thousands of birds for which it is a feeding station during the colder months of the year. Actually the Bay is shared between the counties of Cumbria and Lancashire, the border being at Silverdale. For more than thirty years we have been birdwatching on the Bay and will therefore describe the natural history of the area first before going on to cover the history of the settlements clustered around its shores.

Morecambe Bay is one of Europe's most important ornithological sites with its 120 square miles (192 square km) of sand periodically covered by a shallow sea, and it is an estuary shared by five swift-flowing rivers. The waters of the Lune, Keer, Kent, Leven and Crake cause the gulleys, mud and sandbanks to change position even over a few days, and anyone venturing far on the sands or even wanting to cross should seek the help of the official guide who lives on the Cumbrian side of the Bay. The geology of the area is of great interest as it is very young, having been laid down since the Ice Age, and it has even altered substantially since the sixteenth century when a sinking of the coastline caused a devastating inundation which swallowed up several villages. The fringing rocks vary in colour from startlingly white limestone to red beds of new sandstone, each dominating stretches of the 45-mile (72 km) long coastline.

The Bay itself is a vast expanse of food-rich sand interspersed with exposed areas of dark seaweed-covered rocks called skeers. These provide anchorage for large numbers of mussels which provide food for a number of species of bird, especially gulls and oystercatchers. In addition to the sandbanks and skeers the coastline is fringed with attractive areas of salt marsh dominated by sea purslane, thrift, sea plantain and aster. Before venturing onto these flat areas it is

The gadwall is just one of the many uncommon species of wildfowl which has benefited from the protection given by the RSPB reserve at Leighton Moss.

essential to consult the relevant tide tables. Any tide over 30 feet (9.2 metres) will drive the flocks of waders off their feeding grounds onto the roosts on the higher areas of skeer and salt marsh.

Morecambe Bay is certainly the most important estuary in Britain and may well be Europe's most impressive with high counts of oystercatcher, dunlin, knot, bar-tailed godwit, redshank, curlew, turnstone, lapwing, grey plover, sanderling, golden plover, ringed plover with the occasional grey plover, whimbrel and greenshank. Coordinated counts around the Bay have produced total wader counts of around 250,000 birds, although these are spread over a number of favourite roosting spots.

The wintering population of oystercatchers, whose strident piping calls echo throughout the bay, peaks around 45,000 between August and October, after which some birds continue their journey to the south, leaving a residual population of around 30,000. By late February the return movement to the breeding grounds begins but some 8,000 non-breeding birds are left to summer and there are also a number of pairs which breed on the salt marshes and shingle beaches. Human activities including birdwatching, angling and walking have caused some unintended disturbance to breeding birds and several pairs have moved up the rivers in search of nesting sites on the shingle banks.

Up to 50,000 dunlin winter around the Bay, by the middle of July they are returning from the breeding grounds, and by early August the count may have reached 25,000. The population peaks around the middle of October and the birds remain in the area until April when the return to breeding grounds gets under way. The odd pair remain to nest on the salt marshes and the black belly and reddish upper parts of the breeding bird are much more attractive than the grey-brown winter plumage.

It is the larger, greyer knot, however, which provides the Morecambe Bay bird watcher with the greatest thrill as thousands of birds wheel and twist in orchestrated flight, white underparts flashing even in the faintest flash of sunshine. Up to 80,000 knot winter along the Bay, but in April more than 100,000 may be present as they gather prior to moving north to breed. Some birds remaining towards the end of April show red underparts which contrast sharply with the dark upper surface. Knot do not, however, breed in Britain. The best place for knot-watching is from the area beyond the Hest Bank railway station from the RSPB reserve which is freely open to the public at all times. In very severe weather many knot move off to Walney Island in Cumbria which is probably more sheltered.

Although there are only around 7000 bar-tailed godwits present on the Bay, their distribution is usually more predictable. They tend to concentrate in the Lune estuary area with smaller roosts centred around Hest Bank. Numbers begin to build up towards the end of August, some of the new arrivals still sporting the delightful chestnut breeding plumage. By the end of September the peak population has been reached, the majority of them roosting around Middleton Sands close to the nuclear power station at Heysham. During

March the return migration is in full swing.

Redshank numbers peak at around 13,000 during early October, but the midwinter population is probably around half this figure. Very high tides and windy weather often drive redshanks to feed inland. During March and April most of the birds have moved to their northern breeding grounds, but there is a fairly substantial breeding population in and around the salt marshes fringing the Bay and in the moorland areas which overlook it.

Many curlews use the Bay as a staging post, the mid winter population being around 5,000. Should cold weather strike inland areas of Britain and also northern Europe, curlews pour into the area attracted by the comparative warmth of the sea-washed bay, and numbers can then reach 11,000. The majority have departed by mid-April, but round 2,000 non-breeding birds spend the summer feeding on the rich mudflats.

Turnstones are among the most specialised feeders of all the waders and are confined to shingle areas and mussel beds where they can literally turn over stones in search of food. Around 2,000 birds occur during August and September and again during late April and early May when migration is in full swing. About half this peak population remains throughout the winter, most being concentrated around Heysham and opposite the Broadway Hotel at Morecambe.

Lapwings with their striking black and white plumage and prominent crest earn their alternative name of green plover when struck by shafts of sunlight. Numbers roosting on the Bay vary almost from day to day depending upon prevailing weather conditions. In severe weather almost the entire population heads out over the Bay to Ireland, whilst in mild spells over 6,000 birds may be present. Many pairs breed on the surrounding marshes, fields and moorlands, although there is some evidence to suggest that breeding numbers have declined in recent years. The fields around Cockersand Abbey and Hest Bank are suitable areas for both lapwings and golden plovers of which up to 5,500 can occur around the Bay. In April the golden brown plumage which contrasts sharply with the white underparts becomes less marked as the black belly typical of the breeding bird develops. The delightful grey plover typified by a black patch under the wing is found throughout the Bay, but even at its peak seldom exceeds 250 individuals. Spring tides at Pilling usually yield as many as 20 birds and they also occur fairly frequently around the Lune estuary and around Middleton.

Ringed plovers breed all along the Bay, preferring areas of shingle beach and salt marshes when their furtive running from the nest earns them the local name of 'stone runner'. In May there is quite an impressive migratory movement with as many as 7,500 birds moving through. The return migration in autumn does not seem to be so concentrated and a peak count of 3,000 is more usual. Most birds spend the winter as far south as Africa but around 400 may winter around the Bay. The dainty movements of the ringed plover are perhaps only rivalled by those of the pale-coloured sanderling which can often be seen feeding by running in and out among the waves lapping on the sandy beaches. Their movements are somewhat reminiscent of a clockwork toy, but even at their peak during late August numbers seldom exceed 2,000 birds.

Rarer species include the tall elegant greenshank which occurs around the estuaries of the Kent and Leven during migratory passage particularly during autumn. Whimbrels also occur during spring and autumn, and are often mixed among the flocks of curlew. A likely place to spot whimbrel is on Carnforth marsh.

Other rare species include ruff, little stint, spotted redshank, curlew sandpiper, black-tailed godwit and little ringed plovers, the latter easily distinguished from the common ringed plover by the presence of a bright yellow ring around the eye. Temminck's stint, avocet, dotterel and both grey and red phalarope have also been recorded along the Bay, as have purple sandpipers. This charming little wader demands rocky shores and so is restricted to areas such as Heysham harbour.

Almost the whole shoreline of the Bay is freely open to the public and it is therefore a question of selecting the best vantage points, always remembering to make reference to tide tables.

When the tides are above 25 feet (7.7 metres), the best place to see spectacular wader numbers and their aerial gyrations is Hest Bank salt marshes now administered by the RSPB. The site is reached via the railway crossing leading to a grass verge

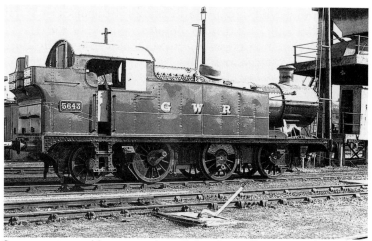

Steamtown provides memories of the days of steam and even the Great Western Railway's heyday is commemorated here.

overlooking the marsh. A small parking fee is charged and there are toilets. Carnforth Salt Marshes are reached via a footpath on the north bank of the River Keer leading from Cote Stones Farm. This leads onto a slag bank, a reminder of the days when iron was smelted here. Now partly grassed over, the area provides a good observation point for waders, being at its best on a tide in excess of 25 feet (7.7 metres), especially in late spring and summer. It is also good for wildfowl, and there is a spectacular gull roost, especially in winter. Carnforth lies on the A5105.

Although Carnforth is the largest settlement on the Lancashire side of the Bay, it is a comparatively modern development and a product of the railway age. It is entirely fitting therefore that Carnforth should be the site of one of the best open-air railway museums in the country.

On display at Steamtown, and signposted from Carnforth centre, are some wonderful old engines still in fine working order, and it is possible to see the *Flying Scotsman* here unless it is away on business. The *Scotsman* was built in 1923 to a design by Sir Nigel Gresley who, in 1937, had an engine named after him.

The LNER, who commissioned the *Flying Scotsman* were so

delighted with both its appearance and performance that it was exhibited at the 1924 British Empire Exhibition. On May 1 1928 it became the first train to travel non-stop between Kings Cross and Edinburgh and it was also the first to average 100 mph for the journey. From 1969 the *Scot* spent three years touring the USA but, thank goodness, she was brought back.

It had not been on regular BR duty since 1963 but had been restored to its apple-green livery and was making money on prestige trips. During its rest periods the *Scot* returns to Steamtown for a spruce-up, which is the finest compliment that the museum could possibly receive.

Actually, Steamtown was a result of a series of happy accidents. Carnforth became an important railway town because the tracks of three railway companies originally met at this point. The Furness Railway Company's Barrow line ran to Carnforth where it connected with the Midland Railway's route to Leeds and the London North Western which operated between Carlisle and London. The companies shared the station, but each had their own sheds, workshops and coaling and watering facilities. Until 1923 the number of railway companies was bewildering, but the system was then somewhat rationalised by the setting up of four major companies – the Great Western, the Southern, the London North Eastern and the London Midland and Scottish. It was the LMS which absorbed Carnforth's three companies.

Faced with three separate and outdated servicing areas, the LMS had to modernise and Carnforth's position made it an ideal centre. The Furness shed, which could service four engines, was replaced in 1938 with a six-road shed complete with a wheel drop and a forge. The building of a locomotive depot was completed in 1942 using Italian prisoners of war as the labour force. When this was complete, Carnforth could coal and water four locomotives in around ten minutes – far quicker and more efficient than anywhere else in Britain. Shortly after the war the railways were nationalised and during the 1950s diesel and electricity began to replace steam.

Three areas in the North did retain steam – the depots at Carnforth, Lostock Hall near Preston and Rosegrove near Burnley. By 1968, however, steam had gone and Carnforth lasted for only one more year as a diesel-engine depot. It was at this time that steam train enthusiasts took over the depot, and Steamtown was born. British Railways in the late 1960s were to ban all steam locomotives from the network, and Steamtown seemed destined to become just an isolated museum. However, in 1972, BR ended their ban when someone with sense recognised the tourist value of 'steam specials'. Steamtown's future was assured, and it now maintains a fleet of engines and rolling stock which is becoming more and more in demand.

If you want to see steam engines built between 1860 and the 1950s, then this is the place to go. If you want to see men who love steam, with engines in bits and being restored, then go to Steamtown.

The museum is open daily, the price varying according to whether all the engines are in steam, only half working or all stock is at rest. There is a model railway, a shop and a cafe. Children can take a short ride on a 15-inch-gauge track pulled by *George V* (built in 1911) and the *Princess Elizabeth* (built in 1914), which both served for many years on the Southport Pier railway.

We often spend an hour in what is called the Mighty Model Railway – not watching the display, splendid though it is, but watching the children aged between 8 and 80 enjoying the 50 locomotives, 150 coaches and 300 waggons whizzing around the display.

This is the real delight of Steamtown. There is something for everyone with an interest in railways, or in the industrial history of Britain.

The railway brought hotels to Carnforth, and therefore it is a good base from which to explore local villages such as Warton, Yealand Conyers and Beetham, and there are also some delightful old houses. One of the finest of these is Borwick Hall.

When William the Conqueror arrived in 1066, he rewarded Roger of Poitou by giving him the lands of the Saxon Earl Tostig which included Borwick. By 1499 Thomas Whittington owned the area, and it was he who built the Pele tower around which the present hall is constructed. After a period under the control of the Redmayne family, Borwick passed to Richard Brindloss who between 1567 and 1590 built extensions which included a magnificent spinning gallery.

Sir Robert Brindloss seems to have been a skilful politician who managed to keep changing sides. How he managed to be created a baronet by Charles I, then be elected a parliamentarian MP in 1650, and then be made County Sheriff between 1671 and 1673 by Charles II defeats us!

The splendid house is now a residential centre run by a Lancashire Youth Clubs Association.

Leaving Carnforth on the Silverdale road leads you first to Steamtown and then in just over one mile to the ancient village of Warton. The surprisingly large parish church dedicated to St. Oswald is overlooked by a sweeping limestone crag. Oswald was the second Christian King of Northumbria, who was converted on the island of Iona off Mull on the west coast of Scotland. In 650 AD he was murdered by the heathen King Penda of Mercia.

The first recorded holder of the benefice of Warton was one William the Chaplain, who was appointed by William de Lancaster as Rector and held office between 1180 and 1189 although none of the present building was then in existence. The oldest part of the church dates from the fourteenth century and is the south aisle which is around 56 feet (17 metres) long. These are probably the dimensions of the medieval church, the present building being around 150 feet (46 metres) long. The visitor to the village cannot fail to be impressed by its cathedral-like size and dominance, but this is not really surprising because it once served all the villages in the area and St. Oswald's is by far the oldest parish.

Once the Normans had imposed their feudal system, Warton became incorporated into the Barony of Kendal. In 1199 John of Anjou – later to become the villainous King John of Magna Carta fame – granted land to Gilbert Fitzreinfride, who was Sheriff of Lancaster between 1206 and 1217. John gave Gilbert the Lordship of Warton and with it the right to hold a market each Wednesday. Here, then, was one of Lancashire's oldest markets, second only to that of Preston, and Warton grew in importance during the thirteenth century.

It was about this time that a branch of the Washington family arrived from County Durham and soon became prosperous and influential. At the top of the hill on Main street and opposite the post office in Washington House, which although

The village of Warton dominated by its cathedral-like church.

rebuilt in the eighteenth century retains the date stone of 1612. Experts feel that the corbelled chimney stack may also have been part of the original building.

Visitors from America find the privately owned house fascinating, but it is the church on which most of their attention is focused. Robert Washington, who died in 1483, paid for the tower to be constructed. His coat of arms was based upon a stars and stripes pattern. This was once carved on the outside of the north wall, but at one time this was plastered over, only to be revealed in 1885 when the plaster flaked off. A pane of glass was then placed over the stone to protect it, but weathering continued until 1955, when the unequal struggle with the elements was abandoned and the stone was removed and taken inside the church. Originally the Washington arms showed 'three mullets and two bars', but even a casual glance at these shows how easy it is to convert them into the American stars and stripes. The genuine American flag which hangs within the church fluttered on top of the Capital building in Washington on 11th May 1966, and was then given to St. Oswald's. It flies from the church tower each 4th of July to celebrate American Independance Day.

Competing with the church as Warton's most historic

treasure is the ruined Old Rectory, now maintained by English Heritage. It was constructed during the fourteenth century when the Scots frequently raided deep into the North West. Many pele towers were constructed during this period and the rectory reflects the architectural skills learned from these structures. The thick walls of the rectory protected the de Thweng family who were related to the Fitzreinfrides. The family, as was the custom in those days, often appointed its sons as rectors of the church and the lords of the manor could also use the rectory as the Court of Justice. Once it ceased to have this dual function, the focus of the court moved to the Malt Shovel Inn now called the Shovel Inn, which was then a combination of inn, solicitor's office and magistrate's court. The Shovel became an important stop on the coach road between Lancaster and Kendal, although in 1792 a more direct turnpike road was constructed cutting out Warton. The final isolation of Warton in the north's communications system was a direct result of the development of Carnforth as a railway junction.

There is a car park signposted 'Old Rectory' from the village centre, and this is also the starting point for a Nature Trail leading up to and around the Crag. The park is on the site of a disused quarry dating back to the time when the Crag was an important source of limestone. This is reflected in the vast number of fossils and also in the variety of plants found along the steep trail. Species found include felwort, marjoram, burnet saxifrage, carline thistle, rock rose, ploughman's spikenard, spring sandwort and the red-seeded dandelion. The tall shrub, purging buckthorn, also occurs here and, as its name implies, it is a powerful laxative – so powerful that is should not be eaten; the black succulent berries which ripen in early autumn are particularly powerful.

There have long been human settlements on and around the Crag; archaeologists have identified Neolithic settlements dating to around 2000 BC and there was a Romano-British tribe based here around AD 200. Aretefacts from both these cultures can be seen in the Lancaster City Museum. Those in search of evidence on the ground should make their way to the summit of the Crag where a hill fort was constructed by a tribe of so-called Ancient Britons who should perhaps be better identified as the Brigantes. The ramparts of the fort can still be seen and the caves they used for burials are still clearly visible. In 1984 the south face of the Crag was declared a nature reserve to be run by a committee with representatives from Lancaster City Council who own the site, Warton Parish Council, the Village Society, the Lancashire Trust for Nature Conservation and the Nature Conservancy Council, and an attractive little trail leaflet has been produced.

Before we leave the village we can never resist spending a few more moments in the churchyard and soaking up a little more history. If one of the greatest of Americans was George Washington, then surely just as high on the British list must be Winston Spencer Churchill. The Kitson family of the now-demolished Warton Hall had a daughter Margaret who married John Washington, and her brother Thomas was born at Warton in 1485 and eventually moved to Hengrave in Sussex. Here he produced a daughter called Katherine who married John Spencer. It was through this branch of the family that Winston Spencer Churchill derived his middle name. Fancy that – George Washington and Winston Churchill actually had a common ancestor!

Although Warton Hall has gone, there is another fine old house between the village and Yealand Conyers which is open to the public. We visited Leighton Hall on a glorious spring day with lesser celendine and primroses shining in the sunlight. Seen on such a day as this, the eighteenth-century house is at its most attractive, blending perfectly into the lush green fields, the hills of Lakeland and Morecambe Bay forming the perfect backdrop. The Hall opens to the public in the summer months although it is closed on Saturdays and Mondays. Tours for parties can be arranged by ringing the Hall, and on some days there are exciting flying displays of birds of prey, and there is an aviary in the gardens of the Hall.

In 1246 the land hereabouts was owned by Adam d'Avranches, and then it passed through several families including the Redmaynes, Yealands, Conyers, Crofts, Middletons, Oldfields, Hodgsons, Towneleys, Worswicks and then to the Gillow furniture family of Lancaster. The present

The thick ruined walls of Warton Rectory. Even the clergy needed stout protection before peace was made with the Scots.

owners, the Reynolds family, are the descendants of the Gillows, and the magnificent furniture within the Hall reflects this.

Leighton Hall was a Catholic house and none was more faithful to King and religion than Sir George Middleton who was a tough cavalier colonel who was knighted and made a baronet on the same day in 1642 whilst with his troop near Durham. Sir George's loyalty to Charles I was remembered by the Cromwellians who heavily fined him.

Albert Hodgson was another owner of Leighton Hall who suffered because of his loyalty to a Stuart king and his religion. He took part in the Jacobite rebellion of 1715 and was captured at Preston. The Government troops did so much damage to the Hall that only a few recognisable indications of its Tudor origins remained.

These were incorporated into the 1763 building in the Adam style and then in 1800 a Gothick-style house was built, the architect probably being Harrison of Chester. There can be few finer houses in Lancashire, and the views from the extensive grounds over to Leighton Moss bird reserve are breathtaking.

The RSPB reserve at Leighton Moss is situated between the

The Shovel – Now a quiet country inn – once a busy coaching inn doubling up as the local courthouse.

villages of Yealand Redmayne and Silverdale, conveniently close to the north-east corner of Morecambe Bay which is now also administered by the RSPB. Although only 128 hectares (320 acres), the reserve has a varied habitat and lies between limestone hills, but the floor is covered with a layer of marine clay and peat. The water draining from this catchment area produces shallow, reed-dominated swamps. Prior to 1917 a pumping system kept a number of farm fields free from water, but once the drainage was stopped for economic reasons the moss was formed. Some of the old farm gates can still be seen sticking up forlornly from the reeds. This is not only an ideal bird habitat, but is one of the finest places in Britain for watching otters.

The problem is to prevent the reeds reducing the area of open water, after which willow and alder would continue the succession towards woodland. The warden's task, therefore, is to cut down the reeds, preferably below the water line, although spraying with carefully selected hebicides has also proved to be effective. Islands have been artificially created, scrapes have been dug out of the soft substratum, and hides have been constructed from which to observe the birds which are attracted to these habitats. An even more impressive variety of birds have been attracted by planting large numbers of native trees including birch, alder, alder buckthorn and guelder rose around the edges.

Apart from the open areas of shallow water (with a maximum depth of just over 0.6 metres – 2 feet), the most important habitat is the 80 hectares (200 acres) of phragmites reed which can stand over 2 metres (6 feet 6 inches) high and thus provide excellent cover. In addition to the fast-growing phragmites, yellow flag, reedmace, bur marigold, great water dock and several sedges also grow. In the damp surroundings meadow sweet, water mint, great willow herb and common spotted orchid all thrive. Above the moss is a fine woodland dominated by oak, ash and birch.

For many years Leighton Moss has been famous for two breeding species, the bittern and the bearded tit. Although affected by harsh winters, as many as 15 pairs of bitterns may breed around Leighton Moss and the adjacent Haweswater, a small reserve administered by the Lancashire Trust for Nature Conservation. The extensive reed beds make the elusive bitterns difficult to observe except when the water is frozen, and then they can be seen walking on the ice. In early spring, however, the booming call of the bittern echoes over the moss and can be heard for miles. It is an eerie sound, especially on a misty morning. Water rails can also be seen during these periods. Bitterns were first recorded at Leighton Moss in the 1940s and were the main reason for the establishment of the reserve in 1964. An important year in the annals of the reserve was 1973 when the bearded tit first bred, since when the population has steadily increased to more than 30 pairs. Other breeding species include mallard, teal, shoveler, pochard, tufted duck and gadwall. The occasional garganey is seen during the summer but breeding has not yet been proved. The spotted crake has, however, occasionally bred among the common residents, the coot, moorhen and lapwing. The shingle areas on the main mere have proved attractive to oystercatchers and common terns, whilst the increasing numbers of piratical black-headed gulls must cause the warden some concern, and they may eventually have to be controlled. The scrub areas attract breeding passerines including whitethroat, lesser whitethroat, grasshopper reed and sedge warblers, reed buntings and redpolls.

In both spring and autumn, passage migrants ensure a constant stream of eager human visitors. In spring, marsh harrier, hen harrier, osprey, purple heron and spoonbill have all been recorded, as have black terns. In autumn ruff, wood and green sandpipers, greenshank and spotted redshank all pass through, whilst starlings, pied wagtails, swallows and sand martins all use the reeds as roosts. The presence of such a food supply attracts sparrowhawk and merlin with the occasional peregrine and hobby. Barn owls also enjoy this food source, and starling bones occur frequently in their pellets.

Predators may also be around in winter, particularly hen harriers on the look-out for the unwary duck which abound at this time. Over a thousand mallard and teal, with pintail, shoveler, wigeon, pochard, tufted duck and goldeneye are all regularly seen. Pink-footed and greylag geese frequently fly over the reserve but seldom land except when the shallow water is frozen. At these times as few as 20 birds can be seen walking round on the ice. Mute swans are resident, whilst occasional flocks of whooper and Bewick swans occasionally appear. The abundance of eels in the shallow water provides food not only for bitterns but also for herons which also prey upon frogs as well as toads and newts which spawn in the lagoons.

There is an information centre at the reserve with a large bookshop. Permits are available on payment at the shop. The reserve is closed on Tuesdays, but there is a public causeway running through the north end of the reserve on which are two public hides, entrance to which is free.

Around a mile from the reserve is Silverdale, now a pleasant little dormitory village which once had an important industrial role. It was a port on the River Kent but was literally left high and dry during the 1920s when the river changed its course and fed into the sea almost four miles away to the west. Wandering down to the beach today past the Silverdale Hotel, it is hard to believe that steamers once tied up here bringing holidaymakers from Morecambe.

There is ample parking on the beach and this is still part of the RSPB area. There is a wader roost providing the tide is in

Leighton Hall – A fine georgian residence built of pale local sandstone.

excess of 25 feet (7.7 metres), and when this reaches 30 feet (9.2 metres) the numbers and movements can be spectacular. The wildfowl counts, especially shelduck and wigeon, are also high, and it is one of the most reliable sites for observing pintail and greylag.

A shoreside footpath leads to Jenny Brown's Point, said to be named after an old woman who lived here in the eighteenth century. The area was once an important centre for copper smelting but all that remains today is a stone smelting chimney. Silverdale was known to the Victorian novelist, Mrs Gaskell, who had a summer house called Lindeth Tower here, and Charlotte Brontë whilst a young girl stayed with friends in the village. We wonder if this is where the literary seed was planted which eventually pursuaded Mrs Gaskell to write the standard biography of Charlotte Brontë. Mrs Gaskell, however, was a well known novelist of her day, her best-remembered work being *Cranford*.

The sea-washed turf from the shoreline has long been in

demand for bowling greens and expensive but instant garden lawns. During the nineteenth century an optimistic plan costing £84,000 was put into operation to build a sea defence and create Dutch-style polder. Unlike the Zuider Zee scheme, however, this faltered, and all that remain today are a few bits of masonry sticking out of the lapping and destructive tide.

This typifies the battle which has gone on for centuries between the Lancashire coastline and the sea, and this is an appropriate point at which to complete this book as we look out over the water into Cumbria.

Further Reading

Bailey, F.A. (1985) *A History of Southport* (Angus Downie)

Collins, H.C. (1953) *Lancashire Plain and Seaboard* (Dent)

Curtis, Bill (1986) *Fleetwood – a town is born* (Terence Dalton)

Davies, Ken (1985) *Windmill Trails of the Fylde* (Scott-Willen)

Freethy, Ron (1983) *A Naturalists' Guide to the Coastline* (David and Charles)

Freethy, Ron (1985) *The River Mersey* (Terence Dalton)

Freethy, Ron (1988) *The River Ribble* (Terence Dalton)

Greenwood, W. (1951) *Lancashire* (Robert Hale)

Hooper, Robin (1988) *The Fylde Story* (Glasgow and Associates)

Lichfield, Patrick Lord (1989) *Blackpool Pleasure Beach through the camera of Lichfield* (Blackpool Pleasure Beach)

Liverpool Heritage Bureau (1978) *Buildings of Liverpool* (Liverpool City Planning Department)

Lytham St. Annes Civic Society (1976) *Lytham St Annes and the Sea* (Civic Society)

Robinson, A. and Millward, R. (1983) *The Shell Book of the British Coast* (David and Charles)

Starkey, H.F. (1983) *Schooner Port* (G.W. and A. Hesketh)

Index

Abbeystead 67-68, 70
Agincourt 102
Ainsdale 20-21
Aintree 1
Alt, river 22
Anfield 1
Ashurst beacon 23
Aughton 20

Baltic sea 47
Banks 23
Bare 119
Barrow-in-Furness 31, 120
Beacon Country Park 23-24
Beetham 133
Big Wheel Cafe 86
Birkdale 27
Birkenhead 2
Blackpool 30, 56, 57-60, 74, 75, 122, 123
Blackpool Tower 23
Borwick Hall 133-134
Bretherton 41
Brighton 30
Bristol 6
Brookhouse 90, 96-98, 101
Burscough Priory 16, 18, 19

Carnforth 130-133, 136
Carr House 40-42, 105
Cartford Bridge 76, 86
Catforth 64
Caton 90, 96-97
Caton Mill 96, 97
Chester 4, 5
Christchurch, Oxford 44
Churchtown (Garstang) 81, 82-83
Churchtown (Southport) 25-27
Cockersand Abbey 96, 108-111, 129
Colne 90
Conder Green 107, 108-109
Cowan Bridge 90
Crake, river 126
Crook-of-Lune 95, 96
Crossens 34-35

Croston 37-38, 42-43
Croxteth 23

Dolphinholme 69-70
Dunsop Bridge 66
Durham 25, 48

Eastham 2
Everton 1, 23

Fairhaven 50, 53-57
Fisherman's Friend 80, 81
Fleetwood 66, 78, 79, 85, 88-89
Flodden 94
Formby 20-21
Freckleton 65
Freshfield 20
Fylde 44ff
Furness Abbey 67

Garstang 72, 76-81
Glasson Dock 90-1, 100, 106, 107-111, 112, 120
Grand National 1
Great Yarmouth 30
Greenhalgh Castle 81-82
Greta, Bridge 93
Greta river 91
Gubberford Bridge 82

Hale 13, 15
Halton 90, 98
Hesketh Bank 33
Hest Bank 128-129
Heysham 87, 115-120, 123, 128
Heysham, power station 114, 115-116
Hoole, Little 41
Hoole, Much 41
Hornby 90, 92-95
Humphrey Head 119

Ince Blundel 27
Ingleton 91
Isle of Man 6, 31, 89, 115

Jenny Brown's Point 142

Keer river 126
Kents Bank 119
Kent, river 126
Kirkby Lonsdale 90, 92
Kirkham 44-48
Knowsley 19, 22-23
Knott End 67, 86-87

Lancaster 42, 45, 90, 98-107, 120
Lancaster canal 73, 79-80. 100, 107
Layton Hall
Leeds to Liverpool Canal 12, 23-24, 27
Leighton Hall 137-139
Leighton Moss 138-141, 142
Leven river 126
Lindisfarne 25
Liverpool 1ff, 30, 41
Liverpool Maritime Museum 11-12
Lune, river 98, 107, 111, 126
Lytham Hall 57
Lytham Mill 46
Lytham St Annes 48-56

Maghull 1
Mains Hall 85
Manchester 30
Marineland 124
Market-Town 81
Marsh Mill 87
Marshaw Wyre 66, 69
Martin Mere 32, 35, 36-39
Marton Mere 60-61
Melling 90, 92
Mere Sands 31, 36, 40
Mersey ferries 3-5
Middleton 130
Middleton holiday camp 114
Milford Haven 4
Morecambe 99, 111, 115, 119-125, 129
Morecambe Bay 31, 126ff

New Brighton 2, 4
North Meols 25

Ormskirk 1, 5, 15-20
Otterspool 13
Overton 111-113
Over Wyresdale 68, 70

Parbold 24
Pier Head 8-10
Port Sunlight 5
Portus Sentantiorum 44, 87
Poulton-le-Fylde 61-62
Poulton-le-Sands 119-120
Preston 32, 41, 43

Rawcliffe Hall 84-85
Ribble estuary 31
Ribble Marshes 32, 33, 34
Ribchester 44
Rivington reservoirs 5, 15
Rosall 27, 84, 88
Rufford 40-41

St Annes see Lytham St Annes
St Annes lifeboat disaster 51-52
St Michaels-on-Wyre 83-84

Scarisbrick 21, 24
Scorton 71-76
Seaforth 10
Sefton 21-22
Shard Bridge 86
Shepherds church 68, 71, 92
Silverdale 126, 141-143
Singleton 61, 62-63
Skelmersdale 23
Skippool 87
Southport 24, 25ff, 48, 133
Speke 13-15
Stannah 87
Steamtown 131-133
Sunderland Point 106, 112-114, 119, 120

Tarleton 41, 42
Tarnbrook Wyre 66, 67
Tewitfield locks 73
Thornbush 108
Thornton 77, 87
Thurnham Hall 109-110
Thurland Castle 91, 92
Torrisholme 119
Tranmere 2
Trough of Bowland 66
Tunstall 90-92

Vale Royal Abbey 44

Wakefield, battle of 94
Walney Island 128

Wardley Creek 86
Warton 133-137
Washington 134-135
Wenning, river 92, 94, 95
Wesham 47
Westminster Abbey 42
Whitehaven 88
Wigan 24, 27, 46
Wirral 2, 4
Woodplumpton 63-64

Wrea Green 44
Wycoller 90
Wyre river 66ff

Yarrow river 42-43
Yealand Conyers 137
Yealand Redmayne 139

Zuider Zee 143